# Slavery, Abortion, and the Politics
# of Constitutional Meaning

For the past forty years, prominent pro-life activists, judges, and
politicians have invoked the history and legacy of American
slavery to elucidate aspects of contemporary abortion politics.
As is often the case, many of these popular analogies have
been imprecise, underdeveloped, and historically simplistic. In
*Slavery, Abortion, and the Politics of Constitutional Meaning*,
Justin Buckley Dyer provides the first book-length scholarly
treatment of the parallels between slavery and abortion in
American constitutional development. In this fascinating
and wide-ranging study, Dyer demonstrates that slavery and
abortion really are historically, philosophically, and legally inter-
twined in America. The nexus, however, is subtler and more
nuanced than is often suggested, and the parallels involve deep
principles of constitutionalism.

Justin Buckley Dyer is an assistant professor in the department
of political science at the University of Missouri–Columbia.
He received a BA in political science and an MPA from the
University of Oklahoma, and an MA and PhD in government
from the University of Texas at Austin. Dyer's research has been
published in *Polity*, *Journal of Politics*, *PS: Political Science and
Politics*, *Politics & Religion*, and *Perspectives on Political
Science*. He is the author of *Natural Law and the Antislavery
Constitutional Tradition* (Cambridge University Press, 2012)
and the editor of *American Soul: The Contested Legacy of the
Declaration of Independence* (2012).

# Slavery, Abortion, and the Politics of Constitutional Meaning

**JUSTIN BUCKLEY DYER**
*University of Missouri–Columbia*

CAMBRIDGE
UNIVERSITY PRESS

CAMBRIDGE UNIVERSITY PRESS
Cambridge, New York, Melbourne, Madrid, Cape Town,
Singapore, São Paulo, Delhi, Mexico City

Cambridge University Press
32 Avenue of the Americas, New York, NY 10013-2473, USA

www.cambridge.org
Information on this title: www.cambridge.org/9781107680746

First published 2013

Printed in the United States of America

A catalog record for this publication is available from the British Library.

Library of Congress Cataloging in Publication Data
Dyer, Justin Buckley, 1983–
Slavery, abortion, and the politics of constitutional meaning / Justin Buckley Dyer.
    pages  cm
Includes bibliographical references and index.
ISBN 978-1-107-03194-4 (hardback) – ISBN 978-1-107-68074-6 (paperback)
1. Abortion – Political aspects – United States.   2. Abortion – Law and
legislation – United States.   3. Slavery – United States.   4. Slavery – Law and
legislation – United States.   5. Constitutional law – United States.   I. Title.
HQ767.5.U5D93   2013
342.73–dc23        2012036929

ISBN 978-1-107-03194-4 Hardback
ISBN 978-1-107-68074-6 Paperback

*For Bennett and Pierce*

# Contents

# Acknowledgments

I am grateful to friends and colleagues who were willing to offer advice and criticism at early stages of this project. Fellow panelists at the 2012 Southern Political Science Association annual conference shared penetrating insights and gave challenging suggestions for the arguments presented in Chapter 5. Stephen Simon and Joshua Hawley pushed back against and sharpened my thoughts on several of the constitutional issues in Chapter 2. J. Budziszewski, Greg Casey, and Gary Jacobsohn each gave meticulous and thoughtful comments on the penultimate draft, and the final product is better for it. Likewise, the counsel I received from the anonymous reviewers at Cambridge University Press has done much to improve the project.

As always, Lew Bateman was a gracious and encouraging editor, and I owe special thanks to his editorial assistants, Anne Lovering Rounds and Shaun Vigil. My colleagues at the University of Missouri have been continually supportive, and I am often struck by how fortunate I am to work where I do. Michael O'Brien, Dean of the College of Arts and Science, and John Petrocik, Chair of the Political Science Department, have fostered an ideal environment for intellectual pursuits. In addition to general support from the college and department, I benefited from the research assistance of Katie Vandermolen and Patrick Shami.

Although many people have had a hand in shaping this book, writing is a solitary affair, and I am sustained in my work by the faces I see when I come home. For her patience and commitment to the demands of academic life, I thank my wife and best friend, Kyle; and for the joy they have brought to our lives, I thank our sons, Bennett and Pierce, to whom I dedicate this book.

# Preface

There is a pervasive feeling among many conscientious citizens that the battle over the institution of slavery in the nineteenth century somehow sheds light on the contours of contemporary American politics. The Supreme Court's landmark decision in *Roe* v. *Wade* (1973), which established a constitutional right to abortion, is repeatedly mentioned in the same breath as the Court's notorious pro-slavery ruling in *Dred Scott* v. *Sandford* (1857). Prominent pro-life politicians and judges routinely accuse opponents of engaging in *Dred Scott*–like legal reasoning, and activists of various stripes proclaim their commitment to a standard of lawfulness that transcends any mere Supreme Court opinion. Meanwhile, many participants in the anti-abortion movement claim to be following in the footsteps of the Great Emancipator, Abraham Lincoln, even as those who resort to violence see themselves as the progeny of the radical abolitionist and domestic terrorist John Brown. For many Americans, the abortion controversy touches a deep nerve, and the search for historical analogs continually leads back to the memory of slavery and abolition.

Similar, perhaps, to the ways in which the legacies of Nazism and Fascism are haphazardly thrown around in our political discourse, many of the contemporary invocations of slavery are, no doubt, sloppy attempts to score partisan points over ideological rivals. Still, slavery and abortion do have a historical, philosophical, and legal nexus in American history. That nexus, however, is subtler and more nuanced than is often suggested, and it is bound up with the meaning and legacy of the Constitution's Fourteenth Amendment, which has become the primary vehicle for the Supreme Court's modern abortion jurisprudence. The story of how an amendment to the Constitution designed to protect the civil rights of newly freed slaves led to the overturning of state abortion laws nearly a century later is complex, to say the least, but one of the key intellectual developments was the rejection of the natural law tradition by influential thinkers in the early twentieth century. For it was the natural law tradition – diverse as it was – that provided the intellectual scaffolding for both the Fourteenth Amendment and state anti-abortion laws (many of which were written during the era of Reconstruction), and it was the rejection of this tradition by the intellectual class that preceded the embrace of abortion rights during the latter half of the twentieth century. The following chapters chronicle the processes of constitutional thought and development that led from the ratification of the Fourteenth Amendment in 1868 to the line of Supreme Court cases inaugurated, a century later, in *Roe* v. *Wade*. The story, however, begins at the end, so to speak, with the complicated life of Norma McCorvey and the ubiquitous sense among many that the current controversies over abortion are somehow illuminated by the history and legacy of American slavery.

I

# The Conscience of a Nation

On an otherwise ordinary morning in the summer of 1970, a divorced and abandoned woman named Pixie went into labor in a Dallas hospital. A self-described "rough woman, born into pain and anger and raised mostly by [herself],"[1] Pixie had spent the last few years as a barker "running the freak show at the Bluegrass Carnival."[2] Though she was young, Pixie had already lived a tough and troubled life, and now, at age twenty-one, she was the mother of three girls born to three different fathers. Her oldest daughter, Missy, was conceived in an abusive and failed marriage she had entered into at age sixteen. Her second daughter, the fruit of a short-lived fling with a young orderly at Baylor University Hospital, was placed for adoption before she woke from the anesthesia. And the child born that morning, she claimed, was the result of a brutal rape.

Young, scared, and alone, Pixie had initially decided after the rape and resulting pregnancy that she didn't "want this *thing* growing inside [her] body" any longer, and, not knowing what the procedure for an abortion was or even what it

---

[1] Norma McCorvey, *I Am Roe: My Life*, Roe *v.* Wade, *and Freedom of Choice* (New York: HarperCollins, 1994), 2.

[2] Ibid., 98.

was called, asked her obstetrician simply to make her "not pregnant."[3] To Pixie's dismay, she was told that in Texas it was illegal to perform an abortion that was unnecessary to save her life, and, admittedly, her life was not in danger.[4] Through a series of events that began with a referral to a Dallas adoption attorney, she then ended up at Columbo's Pizza Parlor seated across from two young, idealistic attorneys searching for a lead plaintiff for a class-action lawsuit challenging the constitutionality of Texas's restrictive abortion law.

In a decision that changed her life, Pixie – whose legal name is Norma McCorvey – agreed to participate. The pregnant, twenty-one-year-old carnival worker assumed the pseudonym Jane Roe in a lawsuit filed against Dallas District Attorney Henry Wade, and nearly three years later – long after McCorvey had given her third daughter up for adoption – the case of *Roe* v. *Wade* was decided in her favor. On January 22, 1973, the Supreme Court of the United States announced in a 7–2 decision that the Constitution protected the right of Jane Roe to terminate her pregnancy, and the Texas law banning elective abortions, along with similar state laws across the country, was deemed unconstitutional.[5]

Yet this landmark decision was fraught with historical ironies. The Jane Roe of *Roe* v. *Wade* never actually had an abortion, and, in fact, she later admitted to fabricating the story about being raped in an attempt to help her case. Perhaps even more confounding, McCorvey now runs a pro-life crisis pregnancy center in Dallas called "Roe No More," and she routinely travels as an anti-abortion activist, even engaging in acts of civil disobedience that led to her recent arrests at Supreme Court Justice Sonia Sotomayor's nomination hearings in Washington, DC, as

---

[3] Ibid., 119.
[4] Texas Penal Code, Articles 1191–1194 and 1196 (1961).
[5] *Roe* v. *Wade* 410 U.S. 113 (1973).

well as at President Barack Obama's 2009 commencement address at the University of Notre Dame.[6] Today, her opposition to abortion runs deep. When called to testify in front of the Senate Judiciary Committee about the consequences of *Roe* v. *Wade*, McCorvey condemned the Court's decision in the strongest possible language. We must ask "Almighty God to forgive us for what we have done," she told the assembled senators. "We must repent for our actions as a Nation for allowing this holocaust."[7] In a turn of phrase that has become common among anti-abortion activists, McCorvey also analogized abortion to slavery in antebellum America. "When slavery was constitutional," she asserted in a statement submitted for the official Senate record, "we treated one class of humans as property. We are treating the humans in the mother's womb as property and less than human when we say it is OK to kill them."[8]

SLAVERY AND ABORTION

Such alleged parallels between slavery and abortion have been a mainstay of American public discourse since 1973, and these analogies have often been drawn at the level of ethics or constitutional interpretation. During his own testimony at the 2005 Judiciary Committee hearings, for example, Ethics and Public Policy Center President Ed Whelan told the senators that the Supreme Court's notorious pro-slavery decision in *Dred Scott* v. *Sandford* (1857) – which, among other things, found a Fifth Amendment constitutional right to traffic in slaves in the federal territories – was the most appropriate historical analog to *Roe*.[9] The landmark

---

[6] Paul Kane, "'Jane Roe' Arrested at Supreme Court Hearing," *The Washington Post* (July 13, 2009); Michael D. Shear, "Cheers, Protests at Notre Dame," *The Washington Post* (May 18, 2009).

[7] Senate Judiciary Committee, *The Consequences of Roe v. Wade and Doe v. Bolton: Hearing before the Subcommittee on the Constitution, Civil Rights, and Property Rights*, 109th Cong., 1st Sess. (June 23, 2005), S-HRG 109-1039, 9.

[8] Ibid., 127.

[9] *Roe* v. *Wade* (invalidating a criminal abortion statute in the state of Texas).

abortion rights case, Whelan insisted, was only "the second time in American history that the Supreme Court has blatantly distorted the Constitution to deny American citizens the authority to protect the basic rights of an entire class of human beings. The first time, of course, was the Court's infamous 1857 decision in *Dred Scott*."[10] In response, Professors R. Alta Charo and Karen O'Connor turned the tables on these appeals to the history of slavery. A judicial decision "overturning *Roe* v. *Wade* would invite states to treat women just as slaves were treated during the pre–Civil War period," Charo submitted[11] before O'Conner expressed her own "worry that the next U.S. Supreme Court case may produce a *Dred Scott*–like case denying women across America their basic constitutional rights to privacy and bodily integrity."[12]

As William Voegeli noted less than a decade after *Roe*, the point of these various analogies "has usually been that the wrong position on abortion treats fetuses – or, conversely, pregnant women – in the same malicious and dehumanizing way as slaves."[13] On one side, advocates of abortion rights argue that the criminalization of abortion is tantamount to legal slavery. "A woman who is forced to bear a child she does not want because she cannot have an early and safe abortion," Ronald Dworkin wrote in his ambitious 1993 book *Life's Dominion*, "is no longer in charge of her own body: the law has imposed a kind of slavery on her."[14] According to this line of reasoning, an unwanted pregnancy is viewed as a kind of forced labor, and opponents of abortion rights are unavoidably depicted as standing on the same moral plane as those who once defended the practice of

---

[10] Senate Judiciary Committee, *The Consequences of Roe v. Wade and Doe v. Bolton*, 25.

[11] Ibid., 28.

[12] Ibid., 43–44.

[13] William Voegeli, "A Critique of the Pro-Choice Argument," *Review of Politics* 43, no. 4 (1981), 563.

[14] Ronald Dworkin, *Life's Dominion: An Argument About Abortion, Euthanasia, and Individual Freedom* (New York: Alfred A. Knopf, 1993), 103.

slavery.[15] Others, such as Northwestern University Law Professor Andrew Koppelman, have gone so far as to argue that the denial of abortion rights is a form of involuntary servitude prohibited by the Thirteenth Amendment.[16] In the rhetoric of abortion rights supporters, *Roe* therefore represents the polar opposite of *Dred Scott*. For critics of constitutional abortion rights, however, the reverse is true. Abortion is depicted as an "evil parallel to that of slavery"[17] – or worse.[18] *Roe*, accordingly, is characterized

---

[15] In a thought experiment, Mark Graber imagines what a society would be like if it truly viewed abortion as a "fundamental human right." In part, Graber suggests that "the pro-life movement" would "be discussed in the same way as *Dred Scott* v. *Sandford* and the pro-slavery movement." See Mark Graber, *Rethinking Abortion: Equal Choice, the Constitution, and Reproductive Politics* (Princeton, NJ: Princeton University Press, 1996), 135. Bruce Ackerman similarly depicts a hypothetical situation in which "extreme pro-lifers" are forced to take a loyalty oath to both the Constitution and *Roe* in the same way Confederates after the Civil War were required to swear fidelity to both the Constitution and "the laws and proclamations" regarding slavery. Bruce Ackerman, *We the People: Transformations* (Cambridge, MA: Harvard University Press, 1998), 139. Implicit in each hypothetical is a moral comparison between pro-slavery and pro-life political movements.

[16] Andrew Koppelman, "Forced Labor: A Thirteenth Amendment Defense of Abortion," *Northwestern University Law Review* 84 (1990), 480. See also Andrew Koppelman, "Forced Labor, Revisited: The Thirteenth Amendment and Abortion," in Alexander Tsesis, ed., *The Promises of Liberty: The History and Contemporary Relevance of the Thirteenth Amendment* (New York: Columbia University Press, 2010), 226–244. For similar arguments submitted in *amicus curiae* briefs, see "Brief for California Committee to Legalize Abortion, et al, as Amici Curiae for Appellants," *Roe* v. *Wade* (*U.S. Supreme Court Records and Briefs, 1832–1978*, Gale/Cengage Learning Document Number: DW108945996) and Brief for Seventy-Seven Organizations Committed to Women's Equality as Amici Curiae in Support of Appellees, *Webster* v. *Reproductive Health Services* 492 U.S. 490 (1989) (1989 U.S. S. Ct. Briefs LEXIS 1511).

[17] Robert P. George, "Law, Democracy, and Moral Disagreement," in Stephen Macedo, ed. *Deliberative Politics: Essays on Democracy and Disagreement* (Oxford: Oxford University Press, 1999), 193.

[18] When asked to write a judicial opinion as though he were on the Court when *Roe* v. *Wade* was decided, Michael Stokes Paulsen asserted: "This [i.e., abortion] is worse than *Dred Scott* and slavery as fire is worse than a frying pan. Slavery is a horrible human wrong. But as bad as it is, murder is worse." See Jack Balkin, ed. *What* Roe v. Wade *Should Have Said: The Nation's Top Legal Experts Rewrite America's Most Controversial Decision* (New Haven, CT: Yale University Press, 2005), 212.

as the "*Dred Scott* of our age,"[19] a decision that threatens the very legitimacy of the American regime because it is a "gross usurpation of the people's authority to act through their democratic institutions to prohibit, or at least, contain" a practice that is fundamentally unjust.[20]

It is within this tense ideological climate that President George W. Bush asserted, in an unscripted moment during the 2004 presidential campaign, that one example of the "kind of person" he would not appoint to the Supreme Court "would be the *Dred Scott* case."[21] As the Washington punditry quickly scrambled to decode Bush's seemingly cryptic remarks, several left-leaning journalists stepped in to explain: "*Roe = Dred*" the title of Katha Pollitt's piece in *The Nation* announced,[22] while Timothy Noah similarly declared in *Slate* that "'*Dred Scott*' turns out to be a code word for '*Roe* v. *Wade*.'"[23] Writing a bit more diplomatically in the *Los Angeles Times*, Peter Wallsten reported that Bush had "a history of using language with special meaning to religious conservatives" before noting the allegation of Bush's critics that "the *Dred Scott* reference was an attempt" to covertly attack abortion rights "without alienating moderates."[24] Of course, for those involved in the American abortion debates it was not much of a revelation that the

[19] Senate Judiciary Committee, *The Consequences of Roe v. Wade and Doe v. Bolton*, 25.

[20] Robert P. George, "Justice, Legitimacy, and Allegiance: 'The End of Democracy?' Symposium Revisited," in Robert P. George and Sotirios A. Barber, eds. *Constitutional Politics: Essays on Constitution Making, Maintenance, and Change* (Princeton, NJ: Princeton University Press, 2001), 322–23.

[21] Transcript of Second Presidential Debate, Washington University, St. Louis, Missouri (October 8, 2004), http://washingtpost.com/wp-srv/politics/debatereferee/debate_1008.html.

[22] Katha Pollitt, "*Roe = Dred*," *The Nation* (November 1, 2004) [posted online October 13, 2004], http://www.thenation.com/article/roe-dred.

[23] Timothy Noah, "Why Bush Opposes Dred Scott: It's Code for *Roe* v. *Wade*," *Slate* (October 11, 2004), http://www.slate.com/articles/news_and_politics/chatterbox/2004/10/why_bush_opposes_dred_scott.html.

[24] Peter Wallsten, "Abortion Foes Call Bush's Dred Scott Reference Perfectly Clear," *Los Angeles Times* (October 13, 2004), http://articles.latimes.com/2004/oct/13/nation/na-dred13.

pro-life movement has long drawn parallels between the issues of abortion and slavery. *The New York Times*, in fact, ran a column just a few days after Bush's remarks in which the Dean of Arts and Letters at Notre Dame predicted that "[h]istory will judge our society's support of abortion in much the same way we view earlier generations' support of torture and slavery – it will be universally condemned."[25] For the last forty years, such rhetorical invocations of slavery in the service of anti-abortion politics have been commonplace.

Writing in *Human Life Review* shortly after *Roe*'s tenth anniversary, President Ronald Reagan laid out what has now become a familiar legal and moral argument against abortion rights. Quoting then-Dean of Stanford Law School (and political liberal) John Hart Ely, Reagan asserted that the Court's opinion overturning state abortion laws in *Roe* v. *Wade* was "not constitutional law and [gave] almost no sense of an obligation to try to be." Reagan continued, perhaps a bit more eloquently than Bush:

> Nowhere do the plain words of the Constitution even hint at a "right" so sweeping as to permit abortion up to the time the child is ready to be born. Yet that is what the Court ruled.
>
> As an act of "raw judicial power" (to use Justice White's biting phrase), the decision by the seven-man majority in *Roe* v. *Wade* has so far been made to stick. But the Court's decision has by no means settled the debate. Instead, *Roe* v. *Wade* has become a continuing prod to the conscience of the nation.[26]

The closest historical parallel to the decision, Reagan suggested, was the fight over slavery in antebellum America and the Supreme Court's attempted resolution of that nationally divisive issue in the case of *Dred Scott* v. *Sandford*. Appealing to the legacy of Abraham Lincoln, and the central role of the Declaration of Independence in Lincoln's statesmanship, Reagan asserted:

[25] Mark W. Roche, "Voting Our Conscience, Not Our Religion," *The New York Times* (October 11, 2004), http://www.nytimes.com/2004/10/11/opinion/11roche. html.

[26] Reagan, "Abortion and the Conscience of the Nation," *Human Life Review* (Spring 1983). http://www.humanlifereview.com/index.php/archives/54-spe cial-archives-spring-1983/.

The great champion of the sanctity of all human life in that day, Abraham Lincoln, gave us his assessment of the Declaration's purpose. Speaking of the framers of that noble document, he said: "This was their majestic interpretation of the economy of the Universe. This was their lofty, and wise, and noble understanding of the justice of the Creator to His creatures. Yes, gentlemen, to all his creatures, to the whole great family of man. In their enlightened belief, nothing stamped with the divine image and likeness was sent into the world to be trodden on. ... They grasped not only the whole race of man then living, but they reached forward and seized upon the farthest posterity. They erected a beacon to guide their children and their children's children, and the countless myriads who should inhabit the earth in other ages."[27]

The egalitarian principles in the Declaration of Independence, Reagan seemed to suggest, were as equally antithetical to the institution of slavery as they were to the practice of abortion, and the various political issues implicated in the nineteenth-century struggle against slavery found striking parallels in the modern fight over the legal status of the unborn.

Reagan's suggestion was not idiosyncratic. The "Letters to the Editor" and op-ed sections of newspapers throughout the world during the last quarter-century attest to a widespread feeling that these two issues are somehow connected. One letter writer to Canada's *The Globe and Mail* asserted in 1985 that the "issue of abortion today closely parallels that of slavery in the nineteenth-century United States," and another, writing more recently in *The Australian*, predicted that "by the end of [the twenty-first] century our society will hang its head in shame at the slaughter of our unborn children from abortion. Like slavery and genocide, our children's children will struggle to comprehend how a civilized society could have allowed such a crime against humanity."[28] At the opening of a museum commemorating the abolition of slavery in England, Charles Moore similarly wrote in London's

[27] Ibid.
[28] William Mathie, Letter to the Editor, "The Heart of the Issue," *The Globe and Mail* (August 10, 1985), A13; Jodie McNeill, Letter to the Editor, *The Australian* (November 4, 2004), 12.

*The Daily Telegraph* that he "found [himself] wondering how abortion will be viewed by museum curators, teachers, historians, and moralists 200 years from now. As the slavery exhibition shows," Moore noted, "something that one generation accepts readily enough is often seen as abhorrent by its descendents – so abhorrent, in fact, that people find it almost impossible to understand how it could have been countenanced in a supposedly civilized society."[29] Writing in *USA Today* during a contentious legislative battle over a proposed national ban on "partial-birth" abortion, Rebecca Hagelin simply asked: "Haven't we learned anything since the struggle to end slavery? The parallels between that battle and the current ugliness surrounding abortion are many."[30]

Among a small cadre of socially conservative intellectuals, comparisons between abortion and slavery have been commonplace as well. Shorty after the decision in *Roe v. Wade*, Amherst College political philosopher Hadley Arkes penned an op-ed piece in *The Wall Street Journal* analyzing the issues at play in *Roe* in light of the celebrated nineteenth-century political debates between Abraham Lincoln and Stephen Douglas.[31] In his 1979 book *A Matter of Choice*, Berkley Law Professor (and later Reagan appointee to the Ninth Circuit Court of Appeals) John Noonan compared the legal dehumanization of slaves in the nineteenth century to the legal dehumanization of the unborn in the twentieth century, suggesting

[29] Charles Moore, "Like the Slave, Is the Unborn Child Not a Man and a Brother?" *The Daily Telegraph* (October 27, 2007), 26.
[30] Rebecca Redd Hagelin, "Don't Stifle Protest," *USA Today* (January 24, 1995), A30.
[31] Hadley Arkes, "The Question of Abortion," *The Wall Street Journal* (October 26, 1976), 26. For a similar discussion, see also George McKenna, "On Abortion: A Lincolnian Position," *The Atlantic Monthly* (September 1995); George Will, "Abortion: Lincoln Can Save the GOP," *The Washington Post* (January 4, 1990), A23; Armstrong Williams, "Abortion and the GOP Whigs," *The Washington Times* (March 29, 1995), A25; William F. Buckley, "Romney's Moral Thought," *National Review Online* (May 12, 2007), http://nationalreview.com/articles/220920/romneys-moral-though/william-f-buckley-jr.

that there has always been "a propensity of professionals in the legal process to dehumanize by legal concepts those whom the law affects harshly."[32] More recently, Robert George – the holder of the prestigious McCormick Chair in Jurisprudence at Princeton University – has argued that abortion resembles slavery "in its denial of the equal dignity of a particular category of human beings,"[33] and Harvard Law Professor Mary Ann Glendon has suggested that the Supreme Court's decision in *Roe*, like *Dred Scott* before it, relied on a "language of dehumanization."[34] For some, abortion is indeed an issue of public morality on par with slavery, and, as a result, *Roe v. Wade* has been cast by at least a few serious thinkers as the *Dred Scott* of our time.

In addition to the copious moral comparisons between slavery and abortion, the technical legal issues at play in *Dred Scott* and *Roe v. Wade* have been the subject of a more direct analogy. In his polemical bestseller *The Tempting of America*, Robert Bork declared that "[w]ho says *Roe* must say ... *Scott*,"[35] and, in a dissenting opinion in *Planned Parenthood v. Casey* (1992), Supreme Court Justice Antonin Scalia explicitly compared the majority's affirmation of the central holding in *Roe* to Roger Taney's *Dred Scott* opinion.[36] Criticism of Chief Justice Taney's argument in *Dred Scott* has, in fact, become somewhat of a proxy for conservative criticism of the Court's abortion jurisprudence. During Senate confirmation hearings for Justice Ruth Bader Ginsburg, Orrin Hatch repeatedly queried Ginsburg about her views on the Court's century-and-a-half–old opinion. "In my view it is impossible," the Utah senator later

---

[32] John T. Noonan, *A Private Choice: Abortion in America in the Seventies* (New York: The Free Press, 1979), 153.

[33] George, "Law, Democracy, and Moral Disagreement," in Macedo, ed. *Deliberative Politics*, 193.

[34] Mary Ann Glendon, "When Words Cheapen Life," *The New York Times* (January 10, 1995), A19.

[35] Robert Bork, *The Tempting of America: The Political Seduction of the Law* (New York: Touchstone, 1991), 32.

[36] *Planned Parenthood v. Casey* 505 U.S. 833, 1001–1002 (1992).

explained, "to distinguish *Dred Scott v. Sandford* ... from the Court's substantive due process/privacy cases like *Roe v. Wade.*"[37] A decade after Ginsburg's confirmation to the Supreme Court, Indiana Representative Mike Pence asserted, with by then familiar rhetoric, that the "reasoning in *Dred Scott* is historically and intellectually almost identical to the reasoning that would be employed in 1973 in a decision known as *Roe v. Wade.*"[38] As a 1973 issue of *Jet* magazine chronicled, the Court's opinion in *Roe v. Wade* was also initially met with criticism "from within Black corners." After the decision in *Roe* was handed down, the Reverend J. H. Jackson, President of the 6-million-member National Baptist Convention, remarked that "the matter of abortions involves the whole scheme of freedom," which, he insisted, must include legal protections for the unborn.[39] Before his eventual embrace of abortion rights during a bid for the presidency in 1984, prominent civil rights leader Jesse Jackson publicly argued that

> If one accepts the position that life is private, and therefore you have the right to do with it as you please, one must also accept the conclusion of that logic. That was the premise of slavery. You could not protest the existence or treatment of slaves on the plantation because that was private and therefore outside your right to be concerned.[40]

Martin Luther King, Jr.'s niece, Dr. Alveda King, has gone even further in invoking the legacy of slavery to describe abortion, telling conservative pundit Bill O'Reilly that

[37] Senate Committee on the Judiciary, *Nomination of Ruth Bader Ginsburg to be Associate Justice of the United States*, 103rd Cong., 1st Sess. (July 22, 1993), S-HRG 103-482, 270. Sen. Hatch also recently had Reagan's 1983 *Human Life Review* essay reprinted in the Congressional Record. See Sen. Orrin Hatch (R-UT), 111th Cong., 2nd Sess., *Congressional Record* (January 22, 2010), S.149-51.

[38] Rep. Mike Pence (R-IN), 108th Cong., 1st Sess., *Congressional Record* (October 8, 2003), H.9366.

[39] "Black Reaction is Mixed to Court OK of Abortion," *Jet* (February 15, 1973), 16-17.

[40] Jesse Jackson, "How We Respect Life is the Overriding Issue," *National Right to Life News* (January 1977). Quoted in Colman McCarthy, "Jackson's Reversal on Abortion," *The Washington Post* (May 21, 1988), A27.

"Slavery is wrong ... [and] that baby – and I know this firsthand – is a slave in the womb of his or her mother."[41]

Even some socially liberal academics and commentators, though not concurring in the conclusion, have implicitly conceded the serious – albeit nuanced – philosophical connection between the issues at play. While considering the notable contention of feminist legal theorist Frances Olsen that "fetal life has value when people with power value it," Harvard Law Professor and liberal legal heavyweight Laurence Tribe responded thoughtfully in his 1990 book *The Clash of Absolutes*, "[t]he same thing was once said of slaves: the value of black Americans was less than the value of white Americans in the view of people with power."[42] Olsen's suggestion – that might makes right – does not set well with most Americans, who have been tutored in a political tradition that emphasizes the equality-in-dignity of all humankind. Whatever the conclusion about abortion, most Americans would prefer to frame the issue around the fundamental principles of human dignity and moral equality rather than mere power politics. And, of course, the metaphor of slavery and the appeal to *Dred Scott* can be (and have been) appropriated for moral and legal defenses of abortion choice.

These various uses of the slavery/abortion analogy are complex, and there is a need for sober analysis devoid of the polemics that so often mar fruitful dialogue about such politically volatile issues. As will become clear as the narrative advances, this book is critically supportive of the pro-life uses of the common analogy between slavery and abortion. The project, however, was also born of a desire to introduce rigorous analysis into the myriad scholarly debates sparked by the comparison – ranging from the development of legal doctrines about substantive due

---

[41] Alveda King, "Personal Story Segment: King's Legacy Continuing," *The O'Reilly Factor* (January 17, 2005).

[42] Laurence Tribe, *Abortion: The Clash of Absolutes* (New York: W.W. Norton & Co., 1990), 119.

process and constitutional personhood (Chapters 2 and 3) to the history of abortion law in light of the slavery analogy (Chapters 4 and 5) to the role of religious arguments in the public square (Chapter 6) and the ethical debates about moral personhood and the tragedy of abolitionist violence (Chapter 7). To even begin to sort through the multi-dimensional analogy between slavery and abortion, however, we must start with the complicated and widely misunderstood case of *Dred Scott v. Sandford* and the relevance it has (and does not have) for the constitutional politics of abortion.

# 2

## Substance, Procedure, and Fourteenth Amendment Rights

Although President Bush's seemingly esoteric reference to *Dred Scott* during a televised debate in 2004 "left many viewers mystified," it was familiar territory for those acquainted with the contours of the American abortion debates.[1] Prominent judges and politicians, from Ronald Reagan and Robert Bork to Antonin Scalia and Orrin Hatch, have long argued that *Roe* v. *Wade* and *Dred Scott* were cut from the same cloth, and, in some quarters, criticism of *Dred Scott* has simply become tantamount to criticism of the Court's general approach to abortion rights. As a matter of constitutional law, the legal doctrine of "substantive due process" – employed in both *Dred Scott* and *Roe* – is particularly troubling to many of the Court's modern detractors. The standard criticism of *Dred Scott* along these lines is that it laid the foundation for the Supreme Court's controversial decision in *Roe* v. *Wade* by illicitly putting a substantive gloss on the Constitution's Due Process Clause so as to strike down a legitimate legislative enactment.

---

[1] Peter Wallsten, "Abortion Foes Call Bush's Dred Scott Reference Perfectly Clear," *Los Angeles Times* (October 13, 2004), http://articles.latimes.com/2004/oct/13/nation/na-dred13.

The Fifth Amendment prohibits the federal government from depriving any person of "life, liberty, or property without due process of law," and on its face the language of the clause seems to be concerned only with the legal procedures by which the government *may* deprive individuals of life, liberty, or property. Yet the Court declared in *Dred Scott* that a legislative act barring slavery from the federal territories "could hardly be dignified with the name due process of law."[2] There was, in other words, a substantive component to the Due Process Clause – in this case, a right to own and traffic in slaves – that was insulated from ordinary legal procedures. Although the Thirteenth Amendment outlawing slavery obviously negated this aspect of *Dred Scott*, several of the post-bellum Court's most controversial decisions have been based on a substantive interpretation of the Fourteenth Amendment's Due Process Clause (which is identical in wording to the Fifth Amendment but applicable against state governments).

Perhaps chief among these controversial decisions is *Roe v. Wade*, a case in which the Court found that the Fourteenth Amendment protects a substantive right to procure an abortion that cannot be unduly burdened by state regulation.[3] For many critics of constitutional abortion rights, the infamous nineteenth-century *Dred Scott* decision (along with other paradigmatic examples of alleged judicial overreach such as *Lochner v. New York*[4]) has become a symbol of anti-democratic judicial politicking and a historical proxy for criticism of *Roe*. According to Judge Bork,

---

[2] *Dred Scott v. Sandford* 60 U.S. 393, 450 (1857) (Taney, C. J.).

[3] The Court found a "right to privacy" in the "Fourteenth Amendment's concept of personal liberty and restrictions on state action" that is "broad enough to encompass a woman's decision whether or not to terminate her pregnancy." See *Roe v. Wade* 410 U.S. 113, 153 (1973) (Blackmun, J.). In *Planned Parenthood v. Casey* 505 U.S. 833 (1992), the Court developed the "undue burden" test to determine whether a provision of law places "substantial obstacles in the path of a woman seeking an abortion" (837).

[4] *Lochner v. New York* 198 U.S. 45 (1905) (striking down sections of a New York State law limiting the number of hours bakers could work in a week).

"[*Dred Scott*] was at least possibly the first application of substantive due process in the Supreme Court, the original precedent for *Lochner* v. *New York* and *Roe* v. *Wade*." *Lochner* employed substantive due process to strike down a state law limiting the hours of work by bakery employees. *Roe* used substantive due process to create a constitutional right to abortion. *Lochner* and *Roe* have, therefore, a very ugly common ancestor. But once it is conceded that a judge may give the due process clause substantive content, *Dred Scott*, *Lochner*, and *Roe* are equally valid examples of constitutional law.[5]

The core of this common critique of *Dred Scott*, *Lochner*, and *Roe* is that the doctrine of substantive due process is inherently at odds with the text and logic of the Constitution's Fifth and Fourteenth Amendments. Any substantive gloss on the meaning of due process is, accordingly, viewed simply as an exercise of will rather than judgment.

As recent scholarship has highlighted, however, the modern critique of substantive due process (and indeed the phrase itself) emerged from the twentieth-century debate over how to reconcile the exercise of judicial power with democratic self-government. In particular, early- and mid-twentieth-century critics of substantive due process took aim at the anti-democratic nature of judicial review – what Alexander Bickel famously termed the "counter-majoritarian difficulty."[6] If the Supreme Court was going to overturn legislation passed by the people's representatives, then its decision had to be grounded in some objective constitutional principle or logic. But substantive due process, the argument went, was unprincipled and ungrounded – a vessel into which the early twentieth-century Court simply poured its own conservative policy preferences. As Keith Whittington explains, twentieth-century "[p]rogressive scholars such as Princeton political scientist Edward Corwin worked hard to identify the 'substantive aspect' of due process doctrine as a recent and

[5] Robert H. Bork, *The Tempting of America*, 32. Bork's quote comes from David Currie, *The Constitution in the Supreme Court: The First Hundred Years: 1789–1888* (Chicago: University of Chicago Press, 1985), 271.
[6] Alexander M. Bickel, *The Least Dangerous Branch: The Supreme Court at the Bar of Politics* (Indianapolis, IN: Bobbs-Merrill, 1962), 16.

misguided judicial innovation, foisted onto the constitutional corpus by a group of conservative policy-oriented judicial activists concerned with defending corporate interests."[7] Corwin's criticism cut both ways, of course, and many post–New Deal judicial scholars have leveled the same charge of policy-oriented judicial activism against the Court's socially libertarian decisions.[8]

On the whole, modern judicial conservatives thus agree with the early progressive critique of substantive due process as unprincipled and ungrounded. Nevertheless, a growing body of interdisciplinary scholarship has painted a more nuanced picture of the late-nineteenth- and early-twentieth-century Court's due process jurisprudence, which was rooted in established antebellum concepts of "class legislation" and the "liberty of contract."[9] Along the way, scholars have highlighted the anachronism of criticizing *Dred Scott*

---

[7] Keith Whittington, "The Troublesome Case of *Lochner*," *Library of Law and Liberty* (blog) (March 1, 2012), http://libertylawsite.org/post/kcith-whittington-the-troublesome-case-of-lochner/. Alexander M. Bickel, *The Least Dangerous Branch: The Supreme Court at the Bar of Politics* (Indianapolis, IN: Bobbs-Merrill, 1962), 16. See, e.g., Edward S. Corwin, "The Doctrine of Due Process of Law Before the Civil War," *Harvard Law Review* 24 (1911), 366, and Charles Groves Haines, "Judicial Review of Legislation in the United States and Doctrines of Vested Rights and of Implied Limitations of Legislatures," *Texas Law Review* 2 (1924), 257 [part 1]; *Texas Law Review* 2 (1924), 387 [part 2]; *Texas Law Review* 3 (1924), 1 [part 3].

[8] See, e.g., Raoul Berger, *Government by Judiciary* (Cambridge, MA: Harvard University Press, 1977) and John Hart Ely, *Democracy and Distrust* (Cambridge, MA: Harvard University Press, 1980).

[9] For a review of recent work that has recovered the concept of class legislation, see generally Gary D. Rowe, "*Lochner* Revisionism Revised," *Law and Social Inquiry* 24 (1999), 221–252 [review of Owen M. Fiss, *History of the Supreme Court of the United States: Troubled Beginnings of the Modern State, 1888–1910*, Vol. 8 (New York: MacMillan, 1993); Howard Gillman, *The Constitution Besieged: The Rise and Demise of Lochner Era Police Powers Jurisprudence* (Durham, NC: Duke University Press, 1993); and Morton J. Horwitz, *The Transformation of American Law, 1870–1960: The Crisis of Legal Orthodoxy* (New York: Oxford University Press, 1992)]. On the "liberty of contract," see, e.g., Charles W. McCurdy, "The 'Liberty of Contract' Regime in American Law," in Harry N. Scheiber, ed., *The State and Freedom of Contract* (Palo Alto, CA: Stanford University Press, 1998), and David Bernstein, *Rehabilitating* Lochner: *Defending Individual Rights Against Progressive Reform* (Chicago: University of Chicago Press, 2011).

on the grounds that it is an exemplar of substantive due process, as we now understand that term. "Prior to the New Deal," Whittington notes, "the phrase 'substantive due process' was practically unknown."[10] Indeed, debate over the *Dred Scott* decision in the nineteenth century centered on a cluster of moral, philosophical, and legal issues that are not easily contained by the phrase "substantive due process," a label designed to draw a sharp distinction between substantive (i.e., moral and philosophical) concerns and clear procedural issues.[11]

There is, to say the least, some ambiguity about how these concepts were employed in the nineteenth century. For example, it was not uncommon for American jurists to conflate "due process of law" with the more familiar phrase "law of the land" contained both in the Magna Carta and in many early state constitutions, and such "law of the land" or "due process of law" provisions were often thought to implicate fundamental principles of justice and substantive limits on government power in addition to procedural protections for criminal defendants.[12] Attention to the early debate about slavery and the Fifth Amendment thus suggests a subtler relationship between *Dred Scott* and

---

[10] Keith Whittington, "The Troublesome Case of *Lochner*."

[11] See, e.g., James W. Ely, "The Oxymoron Revisited," *Constitutional Commentary* 16 (1999), 315–345, and Mark Graber, *Dred Scott and the Problem of Constitutional Evil* (New York: Cambridge University Press, 2006), 63–69. See also Earl M. Maltz, "Fourteenth Amendment Concepts in the Antebellum Era," *American Journal of Legal History* 32 (1988), 317–320, and "*Roe v. Wade* and *Dred Scott*," *Widener Law Journal* 17 (2007–2008), 55–71.

[12] See Ryan C. Williams, "The One and Only Substantive Due Process Clause," *Yale Law Journal* 120 (2010), 408–512 (offering a review of the relevant literature and arguing that a substantive interpretation of due process was part of the historical background against which the Fourteenth Amendment was written). Cf. the reply to Williams by Nathan S. Chapman and Michael W. McConnell, "Due Process as Separation of Powers," *The Yale Law Journal* 121 (2012), 1672–1807. Chapman and McConnell's basic contention (which I do not dispute) is that courts did not hold general and prospective statutes to violate the due process of law in the late eighteenth and early nineteenth centuries.

*Roe* v. *Wade* – one rooted in the moral and theoretical foundations of American constitutionalism.

This is not to say that present concerns about the anti-democratic nature of judicial review are unwarranted or that criticism of judicial philosophizing unmoored from constitutional text and tradition is without merit. It is to say, however, that the narrative of constitutional development fashioned during the Progressive and New Deal eras as a polemic against the *Lochner* Court belies the complexity of constitutional debate and threatens to reduce the contending sides in the debate over *Lochner*, and by extension *Dred Scott* and *Roe*, to advocates of substantive (i.e., moral or philosophical) reasoning, on the one hand, and those faithful to the terms of the original Constitution on the other. Yet moral and philosophical questions were unavoidable in both *Dred Scott* and *Roe*. To take one example (further elaborated in this chapter), the basic threshold question of whether Dred Scott was a citizen of the United States implicated a variety of subsidiary questions about the nature of slavery, the distinction between legitimate and illegitimate property, and the relationship between positive law and natural law. To take another, more obvious example (elaborated in the next chapter), the basic questions in *Roe* about whether unborn human beings are persons and whether choosing to terminate a pregnancy is a basic human liberty implicates a variety of questions about human nature, the value and origins of human life, and the source and scope of fundamental rights.

Substantive interpretations of due process are thus not a novelty in American politics. Modern critics, however, have been correct to point out that the Fourteenth Amendment's Due Process Clause is historically and conceptually a poor medium for many of our current disputes about substantive rights. As we shall see, the Fourteenth Amendment's Privileges or Immunities Clause is a more obvious place to root a discussion of basic justice and civil rights under the Constitution, and a historical caveat is therefore in order: One of the reasons why the Due Process Clause has become central to many of our Fourteenth Amendment debates is that the Supreme Court essentially eviscerated the Privileges or Immunities Clause in a series of cases in the late nineteenth century. As a result, the modern Supreme Court has looked, at times awkwardly, to the Due Process Clause as the primary means to protect fundamental rights. An inquiry into the relationship between *Dred Scott* and *Roe* therefore must both underscore the substantive issues involved in the Court's nineteenth-century due process jurisprudence and highlight the consequences of the Court's early gutting and displacement of the Fourteenth Amendment's Privileges or Immunities Clause. Each of these aspects of early Fourteenth Amendment jurisprudence contributes to the historical and philosophical context of the persistent *Dred Scott/Roe* analogy.

## THE ORIGINS OF THE DUE PROCESS CLAUSE

Nineteenth-century commentators on the American Constitution uniformly traced the Fifth Amendment's protection against deprivations of "life, liberty, or property without due process of law" to Chapter 39 of the Magna Carta, which provided that no freeman would be "captured or imprisoned or disseised or outlawed or exiled or in any way destroyed . . . except by the law of the land."[13] After the American Revolution, many state constitutions contained similar "law of the land" provisions as hedges against arbitrary executive power, and, as Chancellor James Kent wrote, following Coke and Blackstone, "The words, *by the law of the land*, as used originally in Magna Charta" were

---

[13] Magna Carta (1215), Chapter 39, http://www.archives.gov/exhibits/featured_do cuments/magna_carta/translation.html. See, generally, Frederick Mark Gedicks, "An Originalist Defense of Substantive Due Process: Magna Carta, Higher-Law Constitutionalism, and the Fifth Amendment," *Emory Law Journal* 58 (2009), 585–673.

generally "understood to mean due process of law."[14] Even the wording of the Fifth Amendment's Due Process Clause, Joseph Story suggested, "was but an enlargement of the language of Magna Charta. ... So that this clause, in effect, affirm[ed] the right to a trial according to the process and proceedings at common law."[15]

It was unexceptional, however, for American judges and lawyers to argue that the "process and proceedings at common law" also implicated substantive principles. Representing an early strand of what we may be tempted to call "substantive due process," Daniel Webster, for example, argued before the Court in *Dartmouth College* v. *Woodward* (1819) that "Everything which may pass under the form of an enactment is not, therefore, to be considered the law of the land." A merely procedural construction of what constituted "due process," the future senator and secretary of state argued, would "tend directly to establish the union of all powers in the legislature" and render the administration of justice "an idle form, an empty ceremony."

Webster's argument hinged, in part, on a distinction between powers that were "properly legislative" and powers that were judicial or executive in nature. When a legislature engaged in non-legislative acts – for example, by

---

[14] James Kent, *Commentaries on American Law*, ed. Oliver Wendell Holmes, Jr., 12th ed. (Boston, 1896), 2:13. See also Edward S. Corwin, "The Doctrine of Due Process of Law Before the Civil War," *Harvard Law Review*, 24, no. 5 (1911), 366–385. Corwin argues that "law of the land" and "due process" had distinct legal meanings and calls Kent, along with Joseph Story and Thomas Cooley, "willing dupes" for following Sir Edward Coke in his conflation of the two phrases. Nonetheless, Americans understood "due process" to signify the "law of the land" provision in the Magna Carta as it had come to be understood by the eighteenth and nineteenth centuries. See, e.g., Justice Curtis's opinion in *Murray* v. *Hoboken Land Co.* 59 U.S. 272, 276 (1855): "The words 'due process of law' were undoubtedly intended to convey the same meaning as the words 'by the law of the land' in Magna Carta."

[15] Joseph Story, *Commentaries on the Constitution of the United States*, 4th Ed. (Boston: Little, Brown & Company, 1873), Vol. 2, 573. For a discussion of the criminal procedure at common law, see William Blackstone, *Commentaries on the Laws of England: in Four Books* (Philadelphia: R. Welsh, 1902–1915), Vol. 4, 290–354.

passing "acts of attainder, bills of pains and penalties, acts of confiscation, acts reversing judgments, and acts directly transferring one man's estate to another" – it was the proper function of the judiciary to declare the legislative enactment to be contrary to the "law of the land." By defending judicial review of legislative enactments that ran counter to the law of the land, Webster was not conflating procedural norms and substantive norms. Rather, he was suggesting that procedural norms had implicit substantive limitations that were derived from the nature of law itself. In this vein, Webster contended that the legislative act at issue in this case (which dissolved Dartmouth College and reorganized it as a public university by legislative decree) would have been discordant with established constitutional principles *even if "there had been no special restriction on" legislative power* in the United States' Constitution or the Constitution of New Hampshire, because the act was not, strictly speaking, "the exercise of a legislative power."[16]

With respect to vested property rights and the obligation of contracts, some early American judges, particularly at the state level, held similar legislative statutes void under "law of the land" or "due process of law" provisions.[17] Writing contemporaneously with the drafting and ratification of the Fourteenth Amendment, the influential nineteenth-century judge and constitutional lawyer Thomas Cooley gave an overview and summary of the rationale for such judicial action:

> The principles, then, upon which the process is based are to determine whether it is "due process" or not, and not any considerations of mere form. ... When the government, through its established agencies, interferes with the title to one's property, or with his independent enjoyment of it, and its act is called in question as not in accordance with the law of the land, we are to test its validity

---

[16] *Dartmouth College* v. *Woodward* 17 U.S. 518 (1819). Webster's argument before the court is reprinted in *The Great Speeches and Orations of Daniel Webster* (Boston: Little, Brown, & Co., 1886), 1–24.

[17] See generally J. A. C. Grant, "The Natural Law Background of Due Process," *Columbia Law Review* 31 (1931), 56–81, and James W. Ely, "The Oxymoron Revisited," *Constitutional Commentary* 16 (1999), 315–345.

by those principles of civil liberty and constitutional defense which have become established in our system of law, and not by any rules that pertain to forms of procedure merely.[18]

In nineteenth-century America, those principles of "civil liberty and constitutional defense" were, moreover, bound up with the notion of a natural law that set boundaries to legitimate government authority. The natural law tradition, going back to the Roman philosopher and statesman Cicero, had contended that "True law is right reason, harmonious with nature," and the identification of law with "right reason" lived on in the common judicial distinction between "reasonable" and "arbitrary" deprivations of life, liberty, or property.[19] Of course, the simple framing of the problem in terms of reasonable and arbitrary legislation belies the intricacies in the debates about the scope, meaning, and application of due process, and the case of *Dred Scott v. Sandford* provides a powerful illustration of the complexity of these issues in American constitutional politics.

DRED SCOTT AND DUE PROCESS

The controversy in *Dred Scott* began when Scott, a slave under Missouri law, traveled with his master to the free state of Illinois and to the free Wisconsin Territory. Upon returning to Missouri, Scott sued for his freedom, arguing that his extended residence in free jurisdictions manumitted him from his former state of slavery. After a complicated series of events, including a run through the Missouri court system, the Supreme Court took up Scott's case and handed

[18] Thomas Cooley, *A Treatise on the Constitutional Limitations which Rest upon the Legislative Power of the State of the American Union* (Boston: Little, Brown & Co., 1868), 356.

[19] Marcus Tullius Cicero, *The Political Writings of Marcus Tullius Cicero: Comprising his Treatise on the Commonwealth; and his Treatise on the Laws*, trans. Francis Barham, 2 vols. (London: Edmund Spettigue, 1841–1842), Vol. I, Book III, http://oll.libertyfund.org/title/546/83303/1958555. See also Edward S. Corwin, "The 'Higher Law' Background of American Constitutional Law," *Harvard Law Review* 42, no. 2 (1928), 157 (on the influence of Cicero) and 171 (on the idea of "reasonableness" in the common law).

down a decision in March of 1857.[20] The justices issued nine separate opinions, occupying some 240 pages in the *United States Reports*, and scholars still argue about which doctrinal positions commanded the allegiance of a majority of the justices.

Roger Taney's opinion, however, has generally been treated as the opinion of the Court, and two aspects of Taney's argument are particularly of note. On the preliminary question of jurisdiction, the Chief Justice argued that African slaves and their descendents – whether slave or free – were not *and could never become* citizens of the United States.[21] Taney also insisted that the right to own property in slaves was "distinctly and expressly affirmed" in the Constitution and that Congress had no authority to prohibit slave property from entering the federal territories (as it had, for example, in the Missouri Compromise of 1820).[22] The "rights of property are united with the rights of person," Taney explained,

> and placed on the same ground by the fifth amendment to the Constitution, which provides that no person shall be deprived of life, liberty, and property, without due process of law. And an act of Congress which deprives a citizen of the United States of his liberty or property, merely because he came himself or brought his property into a particular Territory of the United States, and who had committed no offence against the laws, could hardly be dignified with the name due process of law.[23]

There was, in other words, a substantive element to the Due Process Clause that prohibited arbitrary legislative interferences with the rights of liberty and property.

As Taney recognized, the contemporaneous criticism of his argument was *not* that the Due Process Clause was merely procedural but rather that the Court failed to

---

[20] For a general history of the case, see Don E. Fehrenbacher, *Slavery, Law and Politics: The Dred Scott Case in Historical Perspective* (New York: Oxford University Press, 1981).

[21] *Dred Scott* v. *Sandford*, 405–6 and 418 (Taney, C. J.).

[22] Ibid., 451 (Taney, C. J.).

[23] Ibid., 450 (Taney, C. J.).

consider adequately the nature of the property in question. "It seems ... to be supposed," Taney conceded, "that there is a difference between property in a slave and other property, and that different rules may be applied to it in expounding the Constitution of the United States."[24] Indeed, Benjamin Curtis, in dissent, asserted that it was "necessary, first, to have a clear view of the nature and incidents of that particular species of property which is now in question," and he insisted that it was "not only plain in itself, and agreed by all writers on the subject, but [was] inferable from the Constitution" that slavery was "contrary to natural right."[25] John McLean, as well, conceded Taney's argument that "every man has a right to go [to the Territories] with his property," but disagreed with Taney's application of this principle to property in human beings. "In this case," McLean noted, "a majority of the court have said that a slave may be taken by his master into a Territory of the United States, the same as a horse, or any other kind of property." While conceding Taney's contention that the Fifth Amendment offered substantive protections for property rights, McLean asserted that slaves were not a species of property held rightfully because they were, by nature, "not mere chattel."[26]

The Republican Party in general, and Abraham Lincoln in particular, also emphasized the moral wrong of owning other human beings rather than taking swipes at Taney's substantive reading of the Fifth Amendment.[27] In a series of debates with Stephen Douglas, Lincoln insisted that "the

---

[24] Ibid., 452 (Taney, C. J.). See Christopher Eisgruber, "*Dred* Again: Originalism's Forgotten Past," *Constitutional Commentary* 10 (1993), 53: "A substantive interpretation of the Due Process Clause, in other words, gets Taney nowhere until coupled with an obnoxious conception of property, which recognizes property in persons."

[25] Ibid., 625 (Curtis, J., dissenting).

[26] Ibid., 550 (McLean, J., dissenting). On this point, see Mark Graber, *Dred Scott and the Problem of Constitutional Evil*, 62.

[27] See Earl Maltz, *The Fourteenth Amendment and the Law of the Constitution* (Durham, NC: Carolina Academic Press, 2003), 7–8. George Thomas points out: "While the due process argument advanced by Roger Taney came to be

fault [with the *Dred Scott* opinion] is not in the reasoning; but the falsehood in fact is a fault of the premises."[28] In this vein, Lincoln disputed Taney's dubious premise that the right to property in a slave was "distinctly and expressly affirmed in the Constitution," but this point rested on a moral and constitutional distinction between ordinary property and slave property. "When [Douglas] says that slave property and horse and hog property are alike to be allowed to go into the territories, upon the principles of equality," Lincoln asserted, "he is reasoning truly, if there is no difference between them as property; but if the one is property, held rightfully, and the other is wrong, then there is no equality between the right and the wrong."[29]

Where Lincoln found fault with Taney's *Dred Scott* opinion was thus not in its mixing of substance and procedure but rather in its substantive vacuity with regard to the wrong of slavery. "You may turn over everything in the Democratic policy from beginning to end," Lincoln insisted,

> whether in the shape it takes on the statute book, in the shape it takes in the *Dred Scott* decision, in the shape it takes in conversation or the shape it takes in short maxim-like arguments – it everywhere carefully excludes the idea that there is anything wrong in [slavery].
>
> That is the real issue. That is the issue that will continue in this country when these poor tongues of Judge Douglas and myself shall be silent. It is the eternal struggle between these two principles – right and wrong – throughout the world. They are the two principles that have stood face to face from the beginning of time; and will ever continue to struggle.[30]

The real debate in *Dred Scott*, Lincoln repeatedly declared, was about which principles would ultimately undergird American constitutionalism in the future, and, as early as

criticized in the twentieth century as an invention of substantive due process, it is telling to note that that was not the essence of the Republican criticism against Taney's due process argument." See George Thomas, *The Madisonian Constitution* (Baltimore, MD: Johns Hopkins University Press, 2008), 41.

[28]  Roy P. Basler, ed., *Collected Works of Abraham Lincoln* (New Brunswick, NJ: Rutgers University Press, 1953), Vol. 3, 231.

[29]  Ibid., Vol. 3, 257.

[30]  Ibid., Vol. 3, 315.

1854 (after the passage of the Kansas-Nebraska Act), Lincoln had been urging his listeners to "readopt the Declaration of Independence, and with it, the practices, and the policy, which harmonize with it."[31]

## THE FOURTEENTH AMENDMENT AND FUNDAMENTAL RIGHTS

As Lincoln had predicted, debate over the fundamental principles of American government did continue long after his tongue and the tongue of Stephen Douglas fell silent. When the Reconstruction Congress set out to pass national civil rights legislation and draft a constitutional amendment in 1866 – both, in part, to overturn various aspects of the *Dred Scott* decision – there was a continuation of those debates about the nature of man and the principles of a free society that had started before the war. For members of the 39th Congress, the problem of civil rights was inseparable from the problem of slavery, and the fundamental rights of human nature were often defined in relationship to what the system of slavery had deprived. As Sen. Jacob Howard (R-MI) noted, the "history of [the previous] two hundred years" had taught that a slave

> had no rights, nor nothing which he could call his own. He had not the right to become a husband or a father in the eye of the law, he had no child, he was not at liberty to indulge the natural affections of the human heart for children, for wife, or even for friend. He owned no property, because the law prohibited him. He could not take real or personal estate either by sale, by grant, or by descent or inheritance. He did not own the bread he earned and ate. He stood upon the face of the earth completely isolated from the society in which he happened to be; he was nothing but a chattel, subject to the will of his owner, and unprotected in his rights by the law of the State where he happened to live.[32]

---

[31] Ibid., Vol. 2, 276.
[32] Sen. Jacob Howard (R-MI), *Congressional Globe*, 39th Congress (30 January 1866), S. 504.

The universal rights of freemen, on the other hand, were often described as the inalienable rights to "life, liberty, and the pursuit of happiness" appealed to in the Declaration of Independence, and, as Sen. Lyman Trumball (R-IL) declared, it was "the intention of this [civil rights] bill to secure those rights" to the "millions of the African race in this country who were ground down and degraded and subjected to a slavery more intolerable than the world ever knew."[33]

In the aftermath of the Civil War, the general application of these broad rights to former slaves was reasonably straightforward. At a minimum, the freedmen would be secured of the

> right to make and enforce contracts, of the right to sue, of the right to be parties and give evidence in courts of justice, of the right to inherit, purchase, lease hold, and convey real and personal property ... [and to have the] full and equal benefit of all laws and proceedings for the security of person and property[.][34]

During legislative debates on the Civil Rights Act of 1866, these rights were described as the "fundamental rights and immunities which are common to the humblest citizen of every free State," and the Fourteenth Amendment, ratified two years later, prohibited states from abridging the privileges or immunities of citizenship or depriving "any person of life, liberty, or property without due process of law."[35]

As Joseph Bradley recognized in a circuit case heard just two years after the Fourteenth Amendment's ratification, one of the primary interpretive questions facing the federal judiciary was whether that amendment was "intended to secure to the citizens of the United States of all classes merely equal rights; or whether it is intended to secure to

---

[33] Sen. Lyman Trumball (R-IL), *Congressional Globe*, 39th Congress (27, 29 January 1866), S. 474.

[34] Rep. Martin Thayer (R-PA), *Congressional Globe*, 39th Congress (2 March 1866) H. 1151–52.

[35] Rep. Martin Thayer (R-PA), *Congressional Globe*, 39th Congress (2 March 1866), H. 1151–52; U.S. Const., amend. XIV.

them any absolute rights."[36] Bradley insisted upon the latter construction, arguing that some absolute rights were among the "privileges or immunities" that the Fourteenth Amendment protected against state abridgment. The recent Court appointee acknowledged that such absolute rights were perhaps "difficult to enumerate or define," but, in a common formulation, Bradley nonetheless suggested that the phrase "privileges or immunities" was shorthand for those fundamental rights lying at "the very foundations of republican government."[37]

In the case immediately at hand, the Louisiana legislature had granted an exclusive right to slaughter animals within the city of New Orleans to the Crescent City Livestock Landing and Slaughter-House Company. Other area butchers, who were required by law to pay a fee to land and slaughter their animals at the Crescent City facilities, claimed that the law was an abridgment of their fundamental right to practice an ordinary vocation free from arbitrary restrictions. Similarly, Bradley framed the constitutional issue as one involving "nothing more nor less than the sacred right of labor," and, although conceding that the legislature may pass a variety of reasonable regulations governing property use or mandating licensing requirements for certain professions, he insisted that a republican government may not create a "corporate or exclusive guild of privileged individuals ... beyond the sacred pale of which

---

[36] *Live Stock Dealers' & Butchers' Association v. Crescent City Live-Stock Landing & Slaughter-House* 15 Federal Cases 649, 650 (1870) (Bradley, J.).

[37] Ibid., 652. The accuracy of Bradley's claim as a matter of original public meaning is, of course, disputed. See, e.g., John Harrison, "Reconstructing the Privileges or Immunities Clause," *Yale Law Journal* 101 (1992), 1385–1474 (arguing that "the main point of the clause is to require that every state give the same privileges and immunities of state citizenship – the same positive law rights of property, contract, and so forth – to all its citizens" [1387–88]). For a nearly diametrically opposed view, see Kurt T. Lash, "The Origins of the Privileges or Immunities Clause, Part I: 'Privileges and Immunities' as an Antebellum Term of Art," *The Georgetown Law Journal* 98 (2010), 1241–1301 (arguing that the Privileges or Immunities Clause "was consistently used as a reference to federally conferred rights and privileges such as those listed in the Bill of Rights" [1299]).

there is no hope of admittance or promotion."[38] On jurisdictional grounds, however, Bradley withheld judgment in the case and signaled the possibility of subsequent review by the Supreme Court.

After consolidating this case with two others involving the contested Louisiana statute, the High Court then took the occasion in the early 1870s to pronounce, for the first time, on the momentous question of whether the Fourteenth Amendment was designed to protect some "absolute rights" – and, if so, what these rights were. Writing for a majority of the Court, Samuel Miller began his opinion in the *Slaughter-House Cases* (1873) by reiterating the classic conception of American federalism. Whereas the national government created by the Constitution of 1787 was a government of limited and enumerated powers, Miller asserted, the states retained broad powers to legislate for the health, safety, and morals of the community. This plenary state power to legislate for the general welfare – commonly referred to as the states' "police power" – was limited, in principle, only by the laws and constitutions of the individual states and by the few restrictions on state governments in the Federal Constitution. One of those federal restrictions, found in Article IV, stipulated that "the Citizens of each State shall be entitled to all Privileges and Immunities of Citizens in the several States."[39] Each state in the Union, in other words, was barred by the terms of the 1787 Constitution from denying a set of common privileges and immunities to out-of-state citizens.

So, what were these "privileges and immunities"? For illustration, Miller turned to a famous and oft-cited opinion delivered by Bushrod Washington, nephew of the first president and an associate justice of the Supreme Court during the Marshall era. "The inquiry," Washington began in an

---

[38] Ibid., 653.
[39] U.S. Constitution, Art. IV, § 1.

opinion for a case involving an obscure New Jersey law that
limited the right to dredge for oysters to state residents,

> is, what are the privileges and immunities of citizens in the several
> states? We feel no hesitation in confining these expressions to those
> privileges and immunities which are, in their nature, fundamental;
> which belong, of right, to the citizens of all free governments; and
> which have, at all times, been enjoyed by the citizens of the several
> states which compose this Union, from the time of their becoming
> free, independent, and sovereign.

These "fundamental principles" were perhaps "more tedious
than difficult to enumerate," but they could nonetheless

> be all comprehended under the following heads: Protection by the
> government; the enjoyment of life and liberty, with the right to
> acquire and possess property of every kind, and to pursue and
> obtain happiness and safety; subject nevertheless to such restraints
> as the government may justly prescribe for the general good for the
> whole. The right of a citizen of one state to pass through, or to
> reside in any other state, for purposes of trade, agriculture, profes-
> sional pursuits, or otherwise; to claim the benefit of the writ of
> habeas corpus; to institute and maintain actions of any kind in the
> courts of the state; to take, hold and dispose of property, either real
> or personal; and an exemption from higher taxes or impositions
> than are paid by the other citizens of the state; may be mentioned as
> some of the particular privileges and immunities of citizens, which
> are clearly embraced by the general description of privileges
> deemed to be fundamental; to which may be added, the elective
> franchise, as regulated and established by the laws or constitution
> of the state in which it is to be exercised. These, and many others
> which might be mentioned are, strictly speaking, privileges and
> immunities, and the enjoyment of them by the citizens of each
> state, in every other state, was manifestly calculated (to use the
> expressions of the preamble of the corresponding provision in the
> old articles of confederation) "the better to secure and perpetuate
> mutual friendship and intercourse among the people of the differ-
> ent states of the Union."[40]

This explication of fundamental rights was, for Washington,
all by way of saying that a state could treat citizens and non-
citizens differently for some purposes – such as the regulation
of fisheries or the dredging of oysters – without running

---

[40] *Corfield* v. *Coryell* 6 Federal Cases 546, 551–52 (1823) (Washington, J.).

afoul of the Constitution. It was only those privileges and immunities "which belong, of right, to the citizens of all free governments" that Article IV of the Constitution sought to secure to all "citizens in the several states."

A similar argument regarding the theoretical basis of both the Civil Rights Act of 1866 and the Fourteenth Amendment appeared over and over again in the debates of the 39th Congress. The major congressional players identified civil rights with natural rights, and Bushrod Washington's famous opinion was repeatedly invoked to buttress the contention that the privileges and immunities protected by the Constitution were those rights "which are in their nature fundamental, which belong of right to the citizens of all free governments."[41] There was, of course, disagreement at the margins about practical application. Were the rights protected by each of the first eight amendments to the Constitution part of the fundamental rights of free men?[42] Could we add to the rights set out in the Bill of Rights the right to vote or the right to enjoy access to public benefits, such as public schooling, without discrimination based on race?[43] Although individual legislators divided on these peripheral questions, there was at least a uniform "understanding that civil rights are the natural rights of man" and these natural rights were uniformly understood in the classically liberal sense of rights to "life, liberty, and property."[44]

---

[41] Sen. Jacob Howard (R-MI), *Congressional Globe*, 39th Congress, 1st session (1866), 2765.

[42] This was, of course, central to the twentieth-century debate about whether the Fourteenth Amendment's Due Process Clause "incorporated" the Bill of Rights. See the appendix to Hugo Black's dissent in *Adamson* v. *California* 332 U.S. 46, 92–123 (1947).

[43] For a discussion of some of these peripheral debates in the 39th Congress, see Michael W. McConnell, "Originalism and the Desegregation Decisions," *Virginia Law Review* 81, no. 4 (1995), 947–1140.

[44] Rep. James Wilson (R-IA), *Congressional Globe*, 39th Congress, 1st session (1866), 1117. This is the dominant scholarly understanding. As Randy Barnett writes, "It is not seriously disputed, however, that some time after ratification it came to be widely insisted by some judges, scholars, and opponents of slavery that Article IV was indeed a reference to natural rights. Nor is it disputed that, whenever

## SLAUGHTER-HOUSE AND CONSTITUTIONAL MEANING

Within the context of American federalism, the foremost practical question was whether the national government had the authority and power to protect the natural rights of citizens in the ordinary administration of government at the local level. Rep. John Bingham (R-OH), the principal architect of Section I of the Fourteenth Amendment, originally raised his own objections to the 1866 Civil Rights Act on precisely these grounds. The "care of the property, the liberty, and the life of the citizen, under the solemn sanction of an oath imposed by your Federal Constitution," Bingham insisted, "is in the States, and not in the Federal Government." "[O]ur Constitution," he continued,

> never conferred upon the Congress of the United States the power – sacred as life is, first as it is before all other rights which pertain to man on this side of the grave – to protect it in time of peace by the terrors of the penal code within organized states; and Congress has never attempted to do it. There never was a law upon the United States statute-book to punish the murderer for taking away in time of peace the life of the noblest, and the most unoffending, as well, of your citizens, within the limits of any State of the Union. The protection of the citizen in that respect was left to the respective States, and there the power is to-day.[45]

Bingham therefore proposed an amendment to the Constitution that would specifically prohibit states from abridging the privileges and immunities of citizens or denying persons – of whatever citizenship or nationality – the due process of law or the equal protection of the laws. To this

it is first developed, the members of the Thirty-ninth Congress meant to import this meaning into the text of the Constitution by using the language of 'privileges' and 'immunities' in the Fourteenth Amendment." Randy E. Barnett, *Restoring the Lost Constitution: The Presumption of Liberty* (Princeton, NJ: Princeton University Press, 2004), 61–62. For a recent revisionist account challenging this consensus, see Nash, "The Origins of the Privileges or Immunities Clause," supra n. 38.

45 John Bingham, *Congressional Globe*, 39th Congress, 1st session (1866), 1291–1293.

was added a new congressional power to "enforce, by appropriate legislation, the provisions of this article."[46]

In the *Slaughter-House Cases*, the Supreme Court was tasked for the first time with determining how transformative the Fourteenth Amendment was for American federalism. What were the fundamental rights protected by the Privileges or Immunities Clause and what was the extent of the new enforcement power conferred upon Congress? Justice Miller began his analysis by noting that the language of the Fourteenth Amendment seemed to make a distinction between national citizenship, on the one hand, and state citizenship on the other. All persons born in the United States, according to the amendment, were citizens of the United States *and* of the state wherein they resided. Miller contended, not implausibly, that state citizenship and national citizenship thus remained distinct under the Constitution. A resident of the national territories could, for example, be a citizen of the United States without being a citizen of a specific state, and by the terms of the amendment no state could abridge the privileges or immunities of "citizens of the United States." The inquiry, Miller maintained, therefore concerned the scope of the privileges and immunities of *national* citizenship as opposed to those of *state* citizenship only.

Like John Bingham, Miller asserted that in the original constitutional order "the entire domain of the privileges and immunities of citizens of the States ... lay within the constitutional and legislative power of the States, and without that of the Federal government." Now, Miller asked,

> Was it the purpose of the fourteenth amendment, by the simple declaration that no State should make or enforce any law which shall abridge the privileges and immunities of citizens of the United States, to transfer the security and protection of all the civil rights which we have mentioned, from the States to the Federal government? And where it is declared that Congress shall have the power to enforce that article, was it intended to bring within the power of

---

[46] U.S. Const. amend. XIV, §5.

Congress the entire domain of civil rights heretofore belonging exclusively to the States?[47]

Bingham's answer would appear to be a qualified "yes." "I have advocated here an amendment," Bingham declared, "which would arm Congress with the power to compel obedience to the oath [to support the Constitution], and punish all violations by State officers of the bill of rights, but leaving those officers to discharge the duties enjoined upon them as citizens of the United States by that oath and by that Constitution."[48] The Fourteenth Amendment, Bingham asserted, neither transferred the entire domain of civil rights to the national government nor kept it, as it had been before the war, in the exclusive jurisdiction of the states. Rather, the amendment prevented the states from abridging the privileges or immunities – understood as natural or fundamental rights – of all citizens while simultaneously granting Congress the power to compel enforcement and punish violations of the article by state officers.

In view of the traditional conception of American federalism, however, Miller insisted that the consequences of such a broad interpretation of the Fourteenth Amendment's Privileges or Immunities Clause would be "so serious, so far-reaching and pervading, so great a departure from the structure and spirit of our institutions" that it would effectively "control and degrade the State governments by subjecting them to the control of Congress, in the exercise of powers heretofore universally conceded to them of the most ordinary and fundamental character" and radically alter "the whole theory of the relations of the State and Federal governments to each other and of both of these governments to the people."[49] Miller offered a less disruptive interpretation, which posited a distinction between those fundamental privileges and immunities protected and guaranteed by the

[47] *Slaughter-House Cases* 83 U.S. 36, 77 (1873) (Miller, J.).
[48] Rep. John Bingham (R-OH), *Congressional Globe*, 39th Congress, 1st session, 1866, 1291–1293.
[49] *Slaughter-House Cases* (1873), 78 (Miller, J.).

states and those protected and guaranteed by the national government. The privileges and immunities of *national* citizenship, Miller asserted, were only those which "owe their existence to the Federal government, its National character, its Constitution, or its laws," such as the right to bring suit in federal courts or make use of federal seaports.[50] Ordinary protections for the life, liberty, and property of citizens were, however, privileges and immunities of *state* citizenship and they remained, as before the war, in the exclusive jurisdiction of state governments.

"The argument," Miller conceded, "was not always the most conclusive which is drawn from the consequences urged against the adoption of a particular construction of an instrument,"[51] but an expansive interpretation of national privileges and immunities – however plausible as a reading of the text – would have essentially destroyed "the main features of the general system."[52] As Walter Murphy suggests, Miller's interpretation of constitutional privileges and immunities seemed to flow "from unstated, and perhaps unconsciously held, major premises about the nature of a constitution and the fundamentality to the American Constitution of federalism as it had been structured before the Civil War."[53] The Fourteenth Amendment, as John Bingham and other framers understood it, amounted, for Miller, to something like an unconstitutional constitutional amendment. In other words, "if fundamental understandings about the federal nature of the Union" were central to the antebellum constitutional order, then "the Fourteenth Amendment, taken at face value, would have effected a revolution in the name of an amendment."[54]

---

[50] Ibid., 79.
[51] Ibid., 78.
[52] Ibid., 82.
[53] Walter Murphy, "*Slaughter-House, Civil Rights*, and Limits on Constitutional Change," *American Journal of Jurisprudence* 32 (1987), 6.
[54] Ibid., 14.

The dissenters, however, viewed the Fourteenth Amendment as a development of, rather than a departure from, the terms of the original constitutional order. Central to this interpretation of the Fourteenth Amendment was a notion of the Declaration of Independence as an enunciation of principles fundamental to the American Constitution. Federalism, imperfect as it was, was a means to secure the natural rights of individuals and to prevent consolidation of power. When antebellum federalism proved ineffectual in securing the rights of newly freed slaves, the means were adjusted to attain the proper ends. This change did not tinker with the fundamental character of the regime but rather maintained continuity with the animating principles of the Declaration, which represented the foundational political act of the American people. The Fourteenth Amendment, Lincoln-appointee Stephen Field maintained, "was intended to give practical effect to the declaration of 1776 of inalienable rights, rights which are the gift of the Creator, which the law does not confer, but only recognizes."[55]

According to Field, the alternative interpretation proffered by Miller and a majority of the Court – that the Fourteenth Amendment intended only to secure *national* privileges and immunities (as opposed to "natural and inalienable rights") – made the article "a vain and idle enactment, which accomplished nothing, and most unnecessarily excited Congress and the people in its passage."[56] With this contention Justice Bradley agreed. The "Declaration of Independence, which was the first political act of the American people in their independent sovereign capacity," Bradley maintained, "lays the foundation of their National existence upon this broad proposition: 'That all men are created equal; that they are endowed by their Creator with certain inalienable rights; that among these are life, liberty and the pursuit of happiness.'" Those natural rights could

[55] *Slaughter-House Cases*, 105 (Field, J., dissenting).
[56] Ibid., 96.

be understood under the general headings of "life, liberty, and property" and they were the core "fundamental rights which can only be taken away by due process of law, and which can only be interfered with, or the enjoyment of which can only be modified, by lawful regulations necessary or properly for the mutual good of all; and these rights, I contend, belong to the citizens of every free government."[57]

Bradley's dissent was a link in the chain connecting early Fourteenth Amendment jurisprudence to antebellum notions of fundamental rights and higher law constitutionalism. According to Bradley, the Fourteenth Amendment was designed to prevent the arbitrary deprivation of natural rights, in part, by prohibiting the abridgment of privileges or immunities of citizenship and proscribing state deprivations of life, liberty, or property without due process of law. Of course, Bradley acknowledged the legitimacy of a wide variety of state regulations of property and labor, but he nonetheless presumed that an arbitrary or class-based piece of legislation would be unfair on its face. Suppose that a state legislature passed a law making the slaughtering of animals a hereditary trade; suppose also that the state charged men with the wrong family surname for opening slaughterhouses in contravention of a legally established caste system. Bradley suggested that the substance of this law would outstrip whatever legitimate procedures were followed and would therefore be an abridgement of one of the fundamental privileges of citizenship (i.e., the right to labor, which flows from the natural right to property) and an arbitrary deprivation of liberty and property under the Fourteenth Amendment's Due Process Clause.

And yet, "even if the Constitution were silent," Bradley contended, "the fundamental privileges and immunities of citizens, as such, would be no less real and no less inviolable than they are now."[58] As Justice Field had occasion to make

[57] Ibid., 116 (Bradley, J., dissenting).
[58] Ibid., 119.

clear in a follow-up case to *Slaughter-House*, this understanding of natural rights presupposed that "just as in our intercourse with our fellow-men certain principles of morality are assumed to exist, without which society would be impossible, so certain inherent rights lie at the foundation of all action, and upon a recognition of them alone can free institutions be maintained."[59] The constitutional provisions dealing with "privileges or immunities" and the "due process of law," the dissenters insisted, were designed to safeguard natural rights to life, liberty, and property and to prevent arbitrary state interference with the exercise of these rights. Justices Bradley and Field further maintained, following the tradition that came before them, that these rights belonged to all persons and that any truly republican government would secure these rights equally to those under its care.

It was thus not only tedious – as Justice Washington had maintained – but perhaps even dangerous to enumerate the privileges and immunities protected by the Constitution. The fundamental rights of citizenship included the natural rights to life, liberty, and property, but their application and security in any particular context required political prudence.[60] It was true that these rights were "absolute" in the sense that they existed independent of and prior to governments and imposed moral obligations on governments; but these rights were always limited by the needs of the common good. The rights to life, liberty, and property might all be taken away without violating the due process of law, and the

---

[59] *Butchers' Union Slaughter-House* v. *Crescent City*, 756–757 (Field, J., concurring).

[60] Although the term *included* natural rights, it was not simply coterminous with natural rights. As Barnett asks, "If the framers of the Fourteenth Amendment meant to protect natural rights – or even civil rights – why did they use the term 'privileges or immunities' instead? The short answer is that they did so because, while 'privileges or immunities' includes natural rights, it is a broader term that includes additional rights." Those additional rights, Barnett suggests, are of the character of those listed in Bushrod Washington's famous 1823 opinion in *Corfield* v. *Coryell*. See Barnett, *Restoring the Lost Constitution*, 61.

exercise of these rights could be regulated in a variety of ways that imposed burdens and protections equally.

## PROPERTY AND SUBSTANTIVE DUE PROCESS

In the late nineteenth century, there was a general sentiment among members of the Supreme Court that fundamental constitutional rights – what were often referred to, following Justice Washington, as the rights that belong to citizens of all free governments – were simply natural rights applied in a particular political context and modified by local regulation and enforcement. As Chief Justice Waite wrote in a case involving a congressional act that made it a national crime to conspire to deprive someone of any right granted under the Constitution,

> The rights of life and personal liberty are natural rights of man. "To secure these rights," says the Declaration of Independence, "governments are instituted among men, deriving their just powers from the consent of the governed." The very highest duty of the States, when they entered into the Union under the Constitution, was to protect all persons within their boundaries in the enjoyment of these "unalienable rights with which they were endowed by their Creator."

The disagreement among members of the Court was not whether natural rights existed or whether they were relevant to constitutional government. Rather, the Court divided over the locus of authority in the American constitutional order for protecting these rights. "Sovereignty, for this purpose," Waite asserted, following *Slaughter-House*, "rests alone with the States."[61]

The decision in the *Slaughter-House Cases* – the first time the Supreme Court was called upon to give a legal construction of the Fourteenth Amendment – had thus greatly limited the scope and application of the Privileges or Immunities Clause. Even so, as Murphy noted, the Court would later

---

[61] *United States* v. *Cruikshank* 92 U.S. 542, 553–4 (1876) (Waite, C. J.). See the Enforcement Act of 1870, *U.S. Statutes at Large*, 41st Congress, 2nd session, Chapter XIV.

compensate for this "surgery on privileges or immunities by expansive readings of due process."[62] Although nationally enforceable fundamental rights were read out of the Privileges or Immunities Clause, the Fourteenth Amendment lived a sort of second life in the late nineteenth and early twentieth centuries as the Court policed state economic regulations under a substantive reading of the Due Process Clause. As Justice Rufus Peckham wrote for the Court in *Allgeyer* v. *Louisiana* (1897), there were certain "inalienable rights relating to persons and property" that were "inherent, although not expressed, in the organic law."[63] A statute that put unreasonable or arbitrary restrictions on the exercise of these inherent rights, Peckham further argued, could "not become due process of law, because it is inconsistent with the provision of the constitution of the Union."[64]

Following one of Justice Bradley's prior formulations, Peckham identified the inherent rights protected by the Fourteenth Amendment's Due Process Clause as the "inalienable rights of freemen" invoked by the Declaration of Independence.[65] Among these was the right to pursue happiness, and this, Bradley had suggested, was a variation of the right to property; it was simply the "right to follow any of the common occupations of life."[66] Similarly, Peckham interpreted the substantive liberty protected by the Fourteenth Amendment primarily in economic terms. "The 'liberty' mentioned in that amendment means," Peckham maintained,

> not only the right of the citizen to be free from the mere physical restraint of his person, as by incarceration, but the term is deemed to embrace the right of the citizen to be free in the enjoyment of all his faculties; to be free to use them in all lawful ways; to live and work where he will; to earn his livelihood by any lawful calling; to pursue

[62] Murphy, "*Slaughter-House, Civil Rights*, and Limits on Constitutional Change," 5.
[63] *Allgeyer* v. *Louisiana* 165 U.S. 578, 585 (1897) (Peckham, J.).
[64] Ibid., 589.
[65] See *Butchers' Union Slaughter-House* v. *Crescent City*, 762 (Bradley, J., concurring).
[66] Ibid., 762.

any livelihood or avocation; and for that purpose to enter into all contracts which may be proper, necessary, and essential to his carrying out to a successful conclusion the purposes mentioned above.[67]

What this meant, in terms of constitutional adjudication, was that states could enact general economic regulations so long as they did not amount to arbitrary or unreasonable interferences with the substantive economic liberty protected by the Fourteenth Amendment.

The much maligned phrase "liberty of contract," which would feature prominently in the debates of the Progressive era, developed from this broad, substantive interpretation of economic liberty, a liberty that "embraced the right to make all proper contracts" as a necessary correlative to "pursuing an ordinary calling or trade, and of acquiring, holding, and selling property."[68] This, in turn, is the jurisprudential tradition out of which the case of *Lochner* v. *New York* emerged at the turn of the century. But contrary to the argument that has been made by Robert Bork and others, there is no straight line from *Dred Scott* to *Lochner* to *Roe*. The historical and legal trajectories are complex, but, as we shall see, *Roe* is more accurately seen as a break with, rather than a continuation of, the natural rights jurisprudence that developed in the first few decades after the ratification of the Fourteenth Amendment.

---

[67] *Allgeyer* v. *Louisiana*, 589 (Peckham, J.).
[68] Ibid., 590.

# 3

# Dred Scott, Lochner, and the New Abortion Liberty

The "judiciary during the *Lochner* era," Howard Gillman notes, "was being faithful to a well-established constitutional tradition."[1] That tradition relied on a distinction "between legitimate promotions of the public interest and illegitimate efforts to impose special burdens and benefits" on discrete groups – a distinction that was often put in terms of reasonable or arbitrary legislative interferences with economic liberty.[2] Determining when state economic regulations were unreasonable was, however, more art than science, and the Old Court had left the "determination to each case as it arises."[3] *Lochner* v. *New York* (1905) was the best-known and perhaps most notorious representative of this line of cases, and the theoretical underpinnings of the Court's majority and dissenting opinions in *Lochner* – rather than those reconstruction debates about slavery and the fundamental rights of free men – have thus largely set the stage for the modern debate about the doctrine of substantive due process.[4] In *Lochner*, the Court ruled unconstitutional a statute enacted by New York legislators

[1] Howard Gillman, *The Constitution Besieged: The Rise and Demise of* Lochner *Era Police Powers Jurisprudence* (Durham, NC: Duke University Press, 1993), 11.
[2] Ibid., 9.
[3] *Allgeyer* v. *Louisiana* 165 U.S. 578, 590 (1897) (Peckham, J.).
[4] *Lochner* v. *New York* 198 U.S. 45 (1905).

that regulated the number of hours bakers were permitted to work in a given week. Justice Rufus Peckham, writing for a majority of the Court and following his own precedent in *Allgeyer* v. *Louisiana*, described what had become the standard jurisprudential approach: "It is a question of which of two powers or rights shall prevail – the power of the State to legislate or the right of the individual to liberty of person and freedom of contract" under the liberty provision of the Due Process Clause. According to this formula, the individual's "right to purchase or sell labor" would be paramount "unless there are circumstances which exclude that right," and Peckham argued that there was "no reasonable ground for interfering with the liberty of person or the right of free contract . . . in the occupation of a baker."[5]

Still, there was some disagreement about the reasonableness of the regulation. Citing two different academic treatises, Justice Harlan noted in dissent that the work of a baker was a physically demanding and potentially hazardous occupation. Long hours, hot ovens, regular inhalation of bread spores, and an irregular sleeping schedule all tasked the health of those working in bakeries, and whether it was reasonable for the state to pass a maximum hours law for this group of workers, Harlan insisted, was a question "about which there is room for debate and for an honest difference of opinion."[6] Although not disputing the general judicial methodology (i.e., striking down unreasonable economic regulations at the state level under a substantive reading of Fourteenth Amendment liberty), Harlan thus disputed the application of the prevailing doctrine in this case.

Harlan's friendly critique of the Court's opinion in *Lochner* has been largely eclipsed by the more provocative dissent tendered by Oliver Wendell Holmes. Justice Holmes was ever the iconoclast, and his *Lochner* dissent was among his more iconoclastic opinions. In now celebrated rhetoric,

---

[5] Ibid., 57 (Peckham, J.).
[6] Ibid., 71 (Harlan, J., dissenting).

Holmes alleged that Peckham had read his own economic theory into the Constitution and reminded his colleagues that "state constitutions and state laws may regulate life in many ways which we as legislators might think as injudicious, or if you like as tyrannical, as this, and which, equally with this, interfere with the liberty to contract." But an individual justice's take on a "particular economic theory, whether of paternalism and the organic relation of the citizen to the State or of laissez faire" was beside the point, for the majority of citizens had a right to "embody their opinions in law." The Constitution, Holmes concluded wryly and with a jab at Peckham's majority opinion, did not "enact Mr. Herber Spencer's *Social Statitcs.*"[7]

It was, of course, true that the Constitution was silent about the social Darwinism of the English sociologist Herbert Spencer, but it was disingenuous to suggest that the Fourteenth Amendment was somehow neutral between socialism and economic liberalism. The amendment was, in large part, an effort to constitutionalize the Civil Rights Act of 1866, and the vision of individual liberty held out in the Civil Rights Act was almost entirely economic. "All persons within the jurisdiction of the United States," the bill stipulated,

> shall have the same right in every State and Territory to make and enforce contracts, to sue, be parties, give evidence, and to the full and equal benefit of all laws and proceedings for the security of persons and property as is enjoyed by white citizens.[8]

For the purposes of the act, the right to "make and enforce contracts" included "the making, performance, modification, and termination of contracts, and the enjoyment of all benefits, privileges, terms, and conditions of the contractual relationship."[9]

[7] Ibid., 75 (Holmes, J., dissenting).
[8] Civil Rights Act of 1866, *United States Statutes at Large*, 39th Congress, 1st session, Chapter XXXI.
[9] Ibid.

The right to set the terms and conditions of one's labor through legally enforceable contracts was thought to be a right "appertaining to every freeman,"[10] and the post-bellum Congress sought to secure this right to former slaves who lived – even after the abolition of slavery – in a state of economic dependence and degradation under southern "black codes." Regardless of what the prevailing view of liberty was in the 1860s, however, Holmes insisted that the word "liberty" in the Fourteenth Amendment was

> perverted when it is held to prevent the natural outcome of a dominant opinion, unless it can be said that a rational and fair man necessarily would admit that the statute proposed would infringe fundamental principles as they have been understood by the traditions of our people and our law.[11]

For Holmes, these fundamental principles – equally compatible with "paternalism" and "laissez faire" and having nothing to say about reasonable or unreasonable economic regulations – were understood quite independent of a theory of natural rights, which had long undergirded the notion of a constitutional "liberty to contract."

While sitting on the Massachusetts Supreme Court, less than a decade before the *Lochner* case was decided, Holmes had delivered a famous address at the Boston University School of Law, taking the natural rights tradition to task and laying the groundwork for what would later develop into the school of "sociological jurisprudence." In his address Holmes urged the assembled students to dispense with the moralism and idealism that had long enveloped legal study and to think of the law simply as the "prophecies" or "systematized prediction" of how the public authority will react in a specific set of circumstances.[12]

---

[10] *Slaughter-House Cases* 83 U.S. 36, 98 (1873) (Field, J., dissenting), quoting Sen. Lyman Trumbull (R-IL) during congressional debates on the Fourteenth Amendment.

[11] *Lochner v. New York*, 75–6 (Holmes, J., dissenting).

[12] Oliver Wendell Holmes, "The Path of the Law," *Harvard Law Review* 10, no. 8 (1897), 458.

This predictive function required lawyers to make an analytical separation between law and morality, for "nothing but confusion of thought can result from assuming that the rights of man in a moral sense are equally rights in the sense of the Constitution and the law."[13] Though there was undoubtedly an overlap between the moral ideas of a particular age and the principles embodied in its laws, the law, in the mind of a lawyer, could only be a prophecy "of what the courts will do in fact."[14] The fundamental principles of the law, alluded to in Holmes' *Lochner* dissent, thus were not substantive moral principles. "For my own part," Holmes confessed, "I often doubt whether it would not be a gain if every word of moral significance could be banished from the law altogether, and other words adopted which should convey legal ideas uncolored by anything outside the law."[15]

Such an analytical separation of law and morality, according to Holmes, would go far in clarifying the work of a judge, which could not involve a procession from foundational axioms or fundamental principles, since "no concrete proposition" – even, incidentally, one espoused by "Mr. Herbert Spencer" – was ever truly "self-evident." In this framework, fundamental legal principles were historically developed ideas that were widely enough diffused in society to yield a reliable prediction about future government action. When there was a prevalent disagreement in some matter of legislative policy, the judge was necessarily handicapped in his predictive capabilities, and the traction gained by socialist ideas in the late nineteenth century was illustrative of this point. As Holmes explained:

> When socialism began to be talked about, the comfortable classes in the community were a good deal frightened. I suspect that this fear has influenced judicial action both here and in England, yet it is certain that it is not a conscious factor in the decisions to which I refer. I think that something similar has led people who no longer

[13] Holmes, "Path of the Law," 460.
[14] Ibid., 461.
[15] Ibid., 464.

hope to control the legislatures to look to the courts as expounders
of the Constitution, and that in some courts new principles have
been discovered outside the bodies of those instruments, which
may be generalized into acceptance of the economic doctrines
which prevailed about fifty years ago, and a wholesale prohibition
of what a tribunal of lawyers does not think about right.[16]

The continued application of legal doctrines based on the
economic ideas of the mid-nineteenth century, Holmes thus
alleged, put judges on one side of "debatable and often
burning questions."[17] Holmes' comments here draw out the
real import of his dissent in *Lochner*, for it represented a
break from the old natural rights tradition and its notion of
a constitutional "liberty to contract." But it was also, in this
vein, a break from the idea at the heart of American constitutionalism that there exist certain self-evident truths that
provide the moral foundation for, and principled limits of,
proper and just government action. As Holmes would later
write in a seminal 1918 *Harvard Law Review* article, "for
legal purposes a right is only the hypostasis of a prophecy –
the imagination of a substance supporting the fact that the
public force will be brought to bear upon those who do things
said to contravene it," and this, Holmes acknowledged,
was much different than "a supposed *a priori* discernment
of a duty or the assertion of a preexisting right."[18]

### FROM *ADKINS* TO *WEST COAST HOTEL*

For the next generation an intra-court battle erupted
between the old natural rights jurisprudence and the new
legal realism as the Court undertook, in a series of cases
involving the liberty of contract, to mark out the constitutional limits of economic regulations under the Due Process
Clauses of the Fifth and Fourteenth Amendments. Central to
the contest was the reasonableness (or unreasonableness) of

[16] Ibid., 467–8.
[17] Ibid., 468.
[18] Oliver Wendell Holmes, "Natural Law," *Harvard Law Review* 32, no. 1 (1918), 42.

state and national laws regulating the hours and wages of employment contracts, and Justice Holmes' *Lochner* dissent emerged, in the midst of the constitutional conflict over Franklin Roosevelt's New Deal, to provide the theoretical foundation for the Court's eventual deference to legislative interferences with economic liberty. Perhaps the two most important cases during this era, which continue to live on in constitutional lore, were *Adkins* v. *Children's Hospital* (1923) and *West Coast Hotel* v. *Parrish* (1937).[19] Each case involved disputed minimum wage laws for women, and the intramural debate over the proper judicial methodology in such liberty of contract cases largely set the stage for the Court's post-war struggle to define the terms of its due process jurisprudence.

Writing for the Court in *Adkins*, George Sutherland acknowledged that "there is, of course, no such thing as absolute freedom of contract," but he insisted that "freedom of contract is, nevertheless, the general rule and restraint the exception, and the exercise of legislative authority to abridge it can be justified only by the existence of exceptional circumstances."[20] Over the dissents of Justices Taft and Holmes, the Court, in this case, held the application of the minimum wage to female employees to be an arbitrary and unreasonable infringement of Fourteenth Amendment liberty. As in his *Lochner* dissent, the general tenor of Holmes' opinion in *Adkins* aimed at the underpinnings and assumptions of the old liberty of contract jurisprudence. The post-bellum Court's Fourteenth Amendment cases, Holmes asserted, began with "an unpretentious assertion of the liberty to follow the ordinary callings" – an "innocuous generality" that was later "expanded into the dogma, Liberty of Contract."[21] But, according to Holmes, the criterion of reasonableness in

---

[19] *Adkins* v. *Children's Hospital* 261 U.S. 525 (1923) and *West Coast Hotel* v. *Parrish* 300 U.S. 379 (1937).
[20] *Adkins* v. *Children's Hospital*, 546 (Sutherland, J.).
[21] Ibid., 568 (Holmes, J., dissenting).

the liberty of contract dogma was, in practice, only the elevation of the policy preferences of the judges over those of the legislators, for in cases such as *Adkins* "a reasonable man reasonably might" think the policy aimed at the common good.[22] Indeed, Holmes signaled his own agreement with the underlying political economy of minimum wage laws and insisted he "could not pronounce an opinion with which [he agreed] impossible to be entertained by reasonable men."[23]

But if all policy issues about which reasonable men could disagree were immune from constitutional challenge, then all policy disputes, it seems, would be resolved in favor of the legislature, since the very act of legislating was evidence that some men – namely, the legislators – thought the policy a reasonable way to combat a particular social evil. But if that were the case, would there be any principled basis for the exercise of judicial review? This was precisely the theoretical challenge the Court faced after its eventual vindication of Holmes' dissent in *West Coast Hotel*. In that case – which later commentators would mark as the inaugural case in a constitutional revolution – a hotel chambermaid in the state of Washington sued for the recovery of unpaid wages under a state minimum wage law for women. The Court took the occasion, in the midst of political turmoil over the constitutionality of the New Deal, to offer a "re-examination of the Adkins Case" and to give a "fresh consideration" of the scope of the police powers of state legislatures.[24] The "violation alleged," Charles Evans Hughes noted for the Court, "by those attacking the minimum wage regulation for women is deprivation of freedom of contract." But, the Chief Justice asked, "What is this freedom? The Constitution does not speak of freedom of contract. It speaks of liberty and prohibits the deprivation of

---

[22] Ibid., 570.
[23] Ibid., 571.
[24] *West Coast Hotel* v. *Parrish*, 390 (Hughes, C. J.).

liberty without due process of law. In prohibiting that deprivation, the Constitution does not recognize an absolute and uncontrollable liberty."[25]

Hughes' framing of the issue in *West Coast Hotel* produced a subtle but important shift in the Court's Fourteenth Amendment jurisprudence, and Justice Sutherland's dissent highlighted the change. In his opinion for the Court in *Adkins*, Sutherland had acknowledged that "there was no such thing as absolute freedom of contract" – an uncontroversial proposition as far as it went. Yet, for the Old Court, represented by Sutherland, "freedom of contract was the general rule and restraint the exception."[26] Hughes' opinion, however, seemed to chart a new course: Deference to legislative judgments about the reasonableness of economic regulations was the rule and exercises of judicial power to overturn infringements of constitutionally protected liberty – especially the unenumerated and amorphous "liberty of contract" – were the exception.

The Court summarized the new jurisprudence the following year in *United States v. Carolene Products* (1938). As Harlan Fiske Stone wrote, the "existence of facts supporting the legislative judgment is to be presumed, for regulatory legislation affecting ordinary commercial transactions is not to be pronounced unconstitutional unless in the light of the facts made known or generally assumed it is of such a character as to preclude the assumption that it rests upon some rational basis within the knowledge and experience of the legislators."[27] In other words, the Court would presume the reasonableness and constitutionality of economic regulations rather than making regulation the exception to the rule of economic freedom. Years earlier and in a different context, Stone gave a fuller exposition of this new methodology. "The vague and general pronouncement of

[25] Ibid., 391.
[26] Ibid., 406 (Sutherland, J., dissenting).
[27] *U.S. v. Carolene Products* 304 U.S. 144, 152 (1938) (Stone, J.).

the Fourteenth Amendment against deprivation of liberty without due process of law," Stone declared,

> is a limitation of legislative power, not a formula for its exercise. It does not purport to say in what particular manner that power shall be exerted. It makes no fine-spun distinctions between methods which the legislature may and which it may not choose to solve a pressing problem of government. It is plain too, that, unless the language of the amendment and the decisions of this Court are to be ignored, the liberty which the amendment protects is not freedom from restraint of all law or of any law which reasonable men may think an appropriate means for dealing with any of those matters of public concern with which it is the business of government to deal.[28]

The test of reasonableness was whether reasonable people might think a given regulation was appropriate, and in the case of economic regulations it was clear that reasonable people were divided about the best policy options. Echoing Holmes' *Lochner* dissent, Stone went on to declare that the "Fourteenth Amendment has no more embedded in the Constitution our preference for some particular set of economic beliefs than it has adopted, in the name of liberty, the system of theology which we may happen to approve."[29] The Constitution, under this framework, remained neutral among competing policy preferences, and the word "liberty," as Holmes had maintained, was perverted when it ran counter to the natural outcome of the dominant opinion in society.

## FOOTNOTE FOUR AND THE SEARCH FOR FUNDAMENTAL RIGHTS

The progressive justices who were instrumental in forging the Court's new judicial methodology soon "came to realize that the removal of traditional restrictions on legislative power not only allowed powerholders to take control of a tumultuous economy and mitigate the social costs of

---

[28] *Morehead v. New York* 298 U.S. 587, 632 (1936) (Stone, J., dissenting).
[29] Ibid., 636.

industrialization, but also to extend power into areas that these reformers considered inviolate."[30] On this point, Stone's contention that the reason the Court should defer to the legislature on regulatory matters was precisely because the Constitution no more enshrined a set of economic principles than it did a system of theology was suggestive, as the analogy with religion brought to the fray its own host of questions. What if a state government adopted a theological program under a sincere and reasonable belief that public piety was related to the health, safety, and morals of the community? On what basis, if any, would the Court strike down this bit of social regulation? Some states, after all, did maintain established churches well into the nineteenth century. Would the Court simply assume that all state and federal legislation was a reasonable exercise of legislative power?

In an initially obscure footnote, Justice Stone anticipated the problem and marked out a possible judicial framework for the principled exercise of judicial review. "There may be narrower scope for operation of the presumption of constitutionality," Stone wrote in what has come to be known simply as Footnote Four,

> when legislation appears on its face to be within a specific prohibition of the Constitution, such as those of the first ten Amendments, which are deemed equally specific when held to be embraced within the Fourteenth. ... It is unnecessary to consider now whether legislation which restricts those political processes which can ordinarily be expected to bring about the repeal of undesirable legislation, is to be subjected to a more exacting judicial scrutiny under the general prohibitions of the Fourteenth Amendment than are most other types of legislation. ... Nor need we enquire whether similar considerations enter into the review of statutes directed at particular religious ... or national ... or racial minorities ... whether prejudice against discrete and insular minorities may be a special condition, which tends seriously to curtail the operation of those political processes ordinarily relied upon to protect

[30] Howard Gillman, "Preferred Freedoms: The Progressive Expansion of State Power and the Rise of Modern Civil Liberties Jurisprudence," *Political Research Quarterly* 47, no. 3 (1994), 623.

minorities, and which may call for a correspondingly more searching judicial inquiry.[31]

Stone's famous footnote suggested that although the Court
would defer to most economic and social legislation, it would
mark off for special judicial scrutiny laws impinging fundamental rights ("such as those in the first ten Amendments"),
obstructing access to the political process (e.g., voting rights),
or invidiously discriminating against vulnerable or politically
powerless groups ("discrete and insular minorities"). Stone,
however, was not the only justice to struggle with the question of how to ground the exercise of judicial power in the
new American state, and no clear consensus emerged to fill
the void left by the demise of the Court's *Lochner*-era
jurisprudence.

As George Thomas explains, there were, instead, "three
central attempts to recast judicial power in light of the
progressive criticism of courts and the New Deal reconstruction."[32] Thomas dubs the first, identified with Justice Stone,
as "democracy-reinforcing," but Felix Frankfurter and
Hugo Black each put forward and defended competing
visions of judicial power. Frankfurter, for his part, advocated a "flexible discovery and articulation of fundamental
values, balanced against the needs of society" and restrained
only by a certain judicial temperament.[33] Judges, on
Frankfurter's "fundamental values" model, would over-
come the New Deal–era problem of limiting judicial power
by exercising a kind of judicial statesmanship, prudentially
deferring to legislatures in some instances and striking down
legislation in others; but the exercise of judicial power
would itself be unbounded by any formulaic and limiting
framework. Leaning far in the other direction, Hugo Black
became a fierce advocate for an explicit, textual basis for the
exercise of judicial review, which, in the context of post-war

---

[31] *U.S. v. Carolene Products* 304 U.S. 144, 155 (1938) (Stone, J.).
[32] George Thomas, *The Madisonian Constitution* (Baltimore, MD: Johns
Hopkins University Press, 2008), 115.
[33] Thomas, *Madisonian Constitution*, 118.

civil liberties jurisprudence, meant a firm adherence and fidelity to the specific terms of the Bill of Rights and deference to state legislatures in all other matters. For Black, the fundamental values jurisprudence of Frankfurter, like Stone's solicitude for a set of preferred freedoms emanating from the nature of the democratic process, "was no different from earlier attempts to protect liberty of contract; it risked equating the values of the justices with the Constitution."[34]

The terms of constitutional debate after 1937 were thus structured, to a large degree, around the rejection of the old natural rights jurisprudence, and the landmark case of *Griswold* v. *Connecticut* (1965) – a forerunner to *Roe* v. *Wade* (1973) – provided a paradigmatic example of the conflicted legacy of the New Deal in the mind of the modern Court. Although the economic substantive due process of the *Lochner* era had long been rejected by the Court, the seeds of a socially libertarian, non-economic version of substantive due process germinated when Estelle Griswold, director of the Planned Parenthood League of Connecticut, challenged a state law banning the "use of any drug or article to prevent conception."[35] Though by mid-century most members of the Court considered anti-contraception laws to be "uncommonly silly"[36] – to parrot Justice Stewart's phrase – the question of whether the law conflicted with the Constitution was another matter, and the post–New Deal Court was ever weary about following in the footsteps of *Lochner*. During oral arguments in *Griswold*, the counsel for the appellant made clear, however, that his clients neither wanted to "revive *Lochner*" nor to "overrule ... *West Coast Hotel*."[37]

[34] Ibid., 119.
[35] *Griswold* v. *Connecticut* 381 U.S. 479 (1965). Some of these non-economic substantive due process cases, including *Meyer* v. *Nebraska* (1925) and *Pierce* v. *Society of Sisters* (1925), are discussed at pp. 482–3 (Douglas, J.).
[36] Ibid., 527 (Stewart, J., dissenting).
[37] Oral argument in *Griswold* v. *Connecticut* (29 March 1965), http://www.oyez.org/cases/1960-1969/1964/1964_496/.

While accepting the invitation to strike down the Connecticut statute, the Court, as well, consciously distanced itself from *Lochner*. Justice Douglas, writing for the majority, acknowledged, "Overtones of some arguments suggest that *Lochner* v. *New York* should be our guide. But," he insisted, "we decline that invitation as we did in *West Coast Hotel*. ... We do not sit as a super-legislature to determine the wisdom, need, and propriety of laws that touch economic problems, business affairs, or social conditions."[38] Even so, Douglas maintained that the anticontraception law operated "directly on an intimate relation of husband and wife and their physician's role in one aspect of that relation," and he grounded the liberty interest in *Griswold* in the "penumbras" that emanate from the specific guarantees in the Bill of Rights and "help give them life and substance."[39]

Douglas' approach followed Footnote Four's suggestion that the specific prohibitions in the Bill of Rights applied against the states by virtue of the Fourteenth Amendment, and his opinion was an elaborate attempt to ground the "right to privacy" in the logic and text of the Constitution's first ten amendments. Justice Goldberg, in a similar vein, wrote separately to breathe new life into the Ninth Amendment with the suggestion that it provided a textual basis for, and evidence of, an unenumerated right to marital privacy. Justices Harlan and Stewart were less patient with the interpretive gymnastics involved in applying against the states unenumerated rights found either in the shadows of the Bill of Rights or in the cryptic terms of the Ninth Amendment. Rather, as Harlan maintained, "the Due Process Clause of the Fourteenth Amendment stands ... on its own bottom."[40] Like Frankfurter, Harlan would look to the fundamental values of our society, which exist quite

---

[38] *Griswold* v. *Connecticut*, 481–2 (Douglas, J.).
[39] Ibid., 484 (Douglas, J.).
[40] Ibid., 500 (Harlan, J., concurring).

independent of the Bill of Rights, and the principal limiting device on judicial power would be a kind of "judicial 'self-restraint,'" rooted in a statesman-like "respect for the teachings of history, solid recognition of the basic values that underlie our society, and wise appreciation of the great roles of the doctrines of federalism and separation of powers have played in establishing and preserving American freedoms."[41] Justice Black, having learned the lessons of 1937, asserted that all of this talk of unenumerated rights, penumbras, and fundamental values was "no less dangerous when used to enforce this Court's views about personal rights than those about economic rights. I had thought," Black protested, "that we had laid that formula, as a means for striking down state legislation, to rest once and for all in cases like *West Coast Hotel*."[42]

Citing a diversity of reasons, seven members of the Court voted to strike down Connecticut's antiquated and largely unenforced law over the objections of Justices Black and Stewart, and the decision, though perhaps uncontroversial as a matter of policy, marked a historic turn in federal civil liberties jurisprudence. In the decade after *Griswold*, the Supreme Court expanded its search for personal rights lying dormant in the shadows of the Constitution, and a more robust non-economic doctrine of substantive due process emerged to form the basis of the Court's controversial abortion rights decision in *Roe v. Wade*. Against this historical backdrop, the Court's foray into abortion politics in the early 1970s was significant for several reasons, not the least of which was its signaling that "the doctrine of substantive due process, thought to be discredited by the Progressive critique of the *Lochner* era, was back. The return of substantive due process and the political reaction to *Roe*," Stephen Griffin explains, "posed a series of urgent

[41] Ibid., 501.
[42] Ibid., 522 (Black, J., dissenting).

questions for constitutional scholars."[43] Those questions required scholars to reflect anew on the principled limits of judicial power, the meaning and substance of due process, and the foundation of constitutional rights. Each of these questions is, in turn, central to the continuing debates in academic constitutional theory, and they lie at the heart of the enduring analogy between slavery and abortion.

## SUBSTANTIVE DUE PROCESS AND THE ABORTION LIBERTY

As Justice Harry Blackmun readily acknowledged in his opinion for the Court in *Roe*, the "abortion controversy" was of a "sensitive and emotional nature," and the moral questions at play inspired "deep and seemingly absolute convictions." Yet such a controversial question, Blackmun contended, had to be resolved by "constitutional measurement, free of emotion and predilection." Very early in his opinion, Blackmun acknowledged that the majority of the Court "[bore] in mind, as well, Mr. Justice Holmes' admonition in his now-vindicated dissent in *Lochner* v. *New York*."[44] The opinion in *Roe*, Blackmun emphasized, was not an attempt to resurrect *Lochner*-era substantive due process. Still, the "principal thrust of [the] appellant's attack on the Texas statutes [was] that they improperly invade[d] a right" protected, in part, by "the concept of personal 'liberty' embodied in the Fourteenth Amendment's Due Process Clause."[45] The burden of the Court in striking

---

[43] Stephen M. Griffin, *American Constitutionalism: From Theory to Politics* (Princeton, NJ: Princeton University Press, 1998), 141.

[44] *Roe* v. *Wade* 410 U.S. 113 (1973), 116–17 (Blackmun, J.).

[45] Ibid., 129 (Blackmun, J.). The Court also entertained arguments based on the Ninth Amendment's reservation of rights to the people but ultimately grounded its decision in the Due Process Clause of the Fourteenth Amendment: "This right of privacy, whether founded in the Fourteenth Amendment's concept of personal liberty and restrictions upon state action, as we feel it is, or, as the District Court determined, in the Ninth Amendment's reservation of rights to the people, is broad enough to encompass a woman's decision whether or not to terminate her pregnancy" (153).

down Texas' abortion law was thus to show how a judicially enforceable right to abortion under the Due Process Clause had a more solid constitutional basis than the liberty to contract at issue in *Lochner*. To use the formula of Holmes' dissent, the Court had to demonstrate that the statute infringed "fundamental principles as they have been understood by the traditions of our people and our law."[46]

For this task, Blackmun "inquired into, and ... place[d] some emphasis upon, medical and medical-legal history," and his opinion rested on the premise that,

> at the time of the adoption of our Constitution, and throughout the major portion of the 19th century, abortion was viewed with less disfavor than under most American statutes currently in effect. Phrasing it another way, a woman enjoyed a substantially broader right to terminate a pregnancy than she does in most States today. At least with respect to the early stages of pregnancy, and very possibly without such a limitation, the opportunity to make this choice was present in this country well into the 19th century.[47]

For evidence of this historical claim, Blackmun relied on the work of New York Law School Professor Cyril Means.[48] In his article "The Phoenix of Abortional Freedom," Means made the novel case ("untold now for nearly a century") that the right to procure an abortion had long been a

---

[46] *Lochner* v. *New York*, 75 (Holmes, J., dissenting).

[47] *Roe* v. *Wade*, 140–141 (Blackmun, J.).

[48] Cyril C. Means, Jr., "The Phoenix of Abortional Freedom: Is a Penumbral or Ninth-Amendment Right About to Arise From the Nineteenth-Century Legislation Ashes of a Fourteenth-Century Common-Law Liberty?" *New York Law Forum* 17, no. 2 (1971), 335–410. In 1971, Sarah Weddington took an end-of-summer vacation at Means' home in Gloucester, Massachusetts, and during oral arguments before the Court she particularly stressed the importance of Cyril Means' work to her argument. Later, Weddington recalled that the justices had copies of Means' article with them at the bench during oral arguments. See David J. Garrow, *Liberty and Sexuality: The Right to Privacy and the Making of* Roe v. Wade (Berkeley: University of California Press, 1994), 503; Joseph W. Dellapenna, *Dispelling the Myths of Abortion History* (Durham, NC: Carolina Academic Press, 2006), 13–14, 689, and 1005 (noting that Blackmun cited Means seven times and cited no other historian except in connection with the history of the Hippocratic oath); and oral argument in *Roe* v. *Wade* (13 December 1971), http://www.oyez.org/cases/1970-1979/1971/1971_70_18/argument. See also *Roe* v. *Wade*, footnotes 26, 33, 41, 47 (Blackmun, J.).

common-law liberty in England and the United States, and he noted that many state abortion statutes were not written until the mid- to late nineteenth century, including the Texas statute written in 1859. This history was "constitutionally significant," according to Means, because

> If every ... Texas woman before 1859, who desired an abortion was at liberty to undergo, and her abortionist at liberty to perform, such a procedure according to the English and American common law, and if all American women (and their abortionists) enjoyed such liberty on September 25, 1789, when the ninth amendment was proposed by the First Congress (in New York City), and on December 15, 1791, when it was adopted, then there is sound ground for holding that such liberty is preserved by that amendment today (subject to abridgment only to promote a compelling secular state interest).[49]

Although Blackmun preferred to ground the abortion liberty in the Fourteenth Amendment rather than the Ninth Amendment, he nonetheless agreed that "a woman enjoyed a substantially broader right to terminate a pregnancy" in the early years of the republic and concluded that the "right to privacy, whether it be founded in the Fourteenth Amendment ... or ... in the Ninth Amendment ... is broad enough to encompass a woman's decision whether or not to terminate her pregnancy."[50]

The state of Texas along with several *amici curiae* put forward the disparate contention that the Fourteenth Amendment protected the right of a fetus to life and that quite apart from the Fourteenth Amendment Texas had a compelling interest in protecting prenatal human life against deliberate destruction. In response, Blackmun laid out an originalist argument that the term "person" in the Fourteenth Amendment had no application before birth, and he claimed that the Court, in adjudicating this controversy, was compelled to strike a posture of neutrality

---

[49] Means, "The Phoenix of Abortional Freedom," 376.
[50] *Roe v. Wade*, 140 and 153 (Blackmun, J.).

regarding the question of "when life begins."[51] By "adopting one theory of life" at odds with the Court's definition of legal personhood, Blackmun concluded, "Texas may [not] override the rights of the pregnant woman" to terminate a pregnancy.[52]

An important part of Blackmun's historical argument was his claim that Texas' therapeutic exception for abortion necessary to save a woman's life belied its own contention that the unborn were full persons. "When Texas urges that a fetus is entitled to Fourteenth Amendment protection as a person," Blackmun wrote in a footnote,

> it faces a dilemma. Neither in Texas nor in any other State are all abortions prohibited. Despite broad proscription, an exception always exists. The exception contained in Art. 1196, for an abortion procured or attempted by medical advice for the purpose of saving the life of the mother, is typical.[53]

As James Witherspoon notes, however, the fact that most nineteenth-century anti-abortion statutes excepted *only* those abortions necessary to preserve the life of the pregnant woman was an "unequivocal indication that these legislatures considered the unborn to be persons in the whole sense."[54] The therapeutic exception was based on established legal principles governing necessary harm that would countenance even the death of "innocent, *born* persons when necessary to avoid a harm that is deemed equal or greater," and, at any rate, the exception was not necessarily inconsistent with "legislative recognition of the personhood of the unborn child."[55]

---

[51] Ibid., 157: "But in nearly all these instances, the use of the word is such that it has application only post-natally. None indicates, with any assurance, that it has any possible pre-natal application." Cf. Means, "The Phoenix of Abortional Freedom," 401–410.

[52] *Roe* v. *Wade*, 162 (Blackmun, J.).

[53] Ibid., 157–8, n. 54.

[54] James S. Witherspoon, "Reexamining *Roe*: Nineteenth-Century Abortion Statutes and the Fourteenth Amendment," *St. Mary's Law Journal* 17 (1985), 46.

[55] Ibid., 47.

Nonetheless, Blackmun's claim that the fetus is a constitutional non-person provided the linchpin for the
Court's decision, because, as Potter Stewart contended
during oral arguments, "if it were established that an
unborn fetus is a person within the protection of the
Fourteenth Amendment," the legal challenge to the Texas
anti-abortion law would be "almost an impossible case."[56]
During the course of questioning, however, members
of the Court seemed to conclude that because unborn
children were not counted for the purposes of representation by U.S. census takers and because the Fourteenth
Amendment confers citizenship on all persons *born* in the
United States, then, as Sarah Weddington urged, "the fetus
prior to birth" is left unprotected by "any kind of federal
constitutional rights."[57] Indeed, in his opinion for the
Court Blackmun insisted that the relevant constitutional
text and history persuasively demonstrated that "the word
'person,' as used in the Fourteenth Amendment, does not
include the unborn."[58]

---

[56] Oral argument in *Roe* v. *Wade* (11 October 1972), http://www.oyez.org/cases/
1970-1979/1971/1971_70_18/reargument. Blackmun acknowledged the same
point in his opinion: "If this suggestion of personhood is established, the
appellant's case, of course, collapses, for the fetus' right to life would then be
guaranteed specifically by the Amendment. The appellant conceded as much on
reargument." *Roe* v. *Wade*, 156–157 (Blackmun, J.).

[57] Ibid.

[58] *Roe* v. *Wade*, 158 (Blackmun, J.). Blackmun's conclusion was based on his
insistence that (a) each use of the word "person" outside of the Fourteenth
Amendment had no application before birth and (b) abortion practices were
"far freer" in the nineteenth century than in 1973. Regarding the first claim,
it is not altogether obvious why this is relevant. To use one of Blackmun's
examples, the Constitution stipulates that to hold the office of president a
"person" must be a natural born citizen, a resident for fourteen years, and
thirty-five years old (U.S. Const., art. II, §1). The language of this provision
would seem to indicate only that a subset of the population of persons is
eligible for the presidency. This offers no independent reason to presume the
word "person" in the Fourteenth Amendment is a legal term of art limited to
those human beings that have been born. In other words, Blackmun cannot
infer his definition of personhood from such provisions.

## THE NEXUS OF *DRED SCOTT* AND *ROE*

It is here, within the discussion of the constitutional definition of personhood, that we find a true resemblance between *Roe* and *Dred Scott*, for in each case the Court excluded some natural human beings from the community of constitutional persons. Though the threshold issue in *Dred Scott* involved the question of Scott's citizenship under the Constitution, the Court treated slaves as non-persons by regarding them as a legitimate species of property protected as chattel to all other persons by the Fifth Amendment. In other words, the Court treated biological human status as irrelevant to the question of constitutional personhood while constructing a legal community of constitutional persons that did not necessarily overlap with the population of natural persons.

It is notable, then, that Cyril Means' article – heavily relied on by Blackmun and Weddington – cited the *Dred Scott* case in particular as an appropriate precedent for at least one aspect of the *Roe* decision. Whether or not the state of Texas considered unborn human beings to be "persons" deserving of legal protection, Means argued, was constitutionally irrelevant because the "Federal Constitution must . . . have a nationwide uniform federal interpretation." An "interesting precedent on this subject," Means acknowledged, was

> the famous case of *Dred Scott* v. *Sanford*, the case decided by the United States Supreme Court in 1857 in which the question that the Court preliminarily had to reach was whether or not the words "Citizens of different States" in the diversity of citizenship clause in Article III of the original Constitution did or did not include a Negro who originally had been a slave, but who had moved to free soil and under the law there enforced became free.
>
> One of the points decided by the Court in that case was that the word "'Citizens" in Article III had to have a uniform nationwide federal meaning which an individual state could not vary. That part of the decision (although not the rest of it, obviously, for the remainder has been reversed by history) is still good law. So no matter what a state could elect to do on the subject, by way of declaring a foetus to be a "person" for some state law purposes, it

could not bind either federal or state courts in interpreting the word "person" in the Federal Constitution.[59]

The Court would soon be tasked with providing a uniform national interpretation for the word "person," and Means urged the *Roe* Court to treat the question in the same manner the Court had treated the question of citizenship in *Dred Scott*.

In the *Dred Scott* case, Justice Taney attempted to define national citizenship by emphasizing what he deemed to be the original intent of the framers. The "legislation and histories of the times, and the language used in the Declaration of Independence," Taney argued, show that slaves and their descendents "were not acknowledged as part of the people nor intended to be included in the general words used in that memorable instrument." Rather, in Taney's now infamous words,

> They had for more than a century been regarded as beings of an inferior order and altogether unfit to associate with the white race, either in social or political relations; and so far inferior that they had no rights the white man was bound to respect; and that the negro might justly and lawfully be reduced to slavery for his benefit.[60]

The apparent asymmetry between the assertion in the Declaration of Independence that "all men are created equal" and "endowed by their Creator with certain unalienable rights" and the practice of race-based chattel slavery was evidence, as well, that the founding document of the

---

[59] Means, "Phoenix of Abortional Freedom," 404. Similarly, Weddington argued that the state of Texas could not define the unborn as a person deserving of protection because "it is up to this Court to make that determination." See oral reargument in *Roe* v. *Wade* (11 October 1972) http://www.oyez.org/cases/1970-1979/1971/1971_70_18/reargument. For a similar argument, see also Ronald Dworkin, "Unenumerated Rights: Whether and How *Roe* Should be Overruled," *The University of Chicago Law Review* 59, no. 1 (1992) 400–401. Dworkin argues that "a fetus is not part of the constitutional population, under the national constitutional arrangement," and, therefore, "states have no power to overrule that national arrangement by themselves declaring that fetuses have rights competitive with the constitutional rights of pregnant women" (401).

[60] *Dred Scott* v. *Sandford* 60 U.S. 393, 407 (1857) (Taney, C.J.).

American regime was "not in any part of the civilized world supposed to embrace the negro race" at the time it was written.[61] American history, according to Taney, indicated that the term "citizen" as it was used in the federal Constitution did not, and *could never*, include African slaves and their descendants.

While acknowledging the significant ways in which the decision was no longer relevant, Means nonetheless aped Taney's general methodology, and he argued that the word "person" in several clauses in the Constitution, such as the clause outlining the basis of representation in the House of Representatives (Art. I § 2, c. 3), showed that those "who had framed the original Constitution and . . . helped to frame the Bill of Rights . . . did not think that a foetus was a person." For additional historical evidence that the framers considered the fetus to be a non-person, Means asserted that "one could do no better than to consult" Samuel Farr's 1787 *Elements of Medical Jurisprudence*, wherein the eighteenth-century English physician asserted the early embryo was "not a human creature" and that "were a child to be born in the shape which it presents in the first stages of pregnancy, it would be a monster indeed, as great as any which was ever brought to light."[62] After citing this text, Means expressed his hope that when the "question is finally argued before the Supreme Court," the "refreshing simplicity" of Farr's description of the early embryo as non-human would outweigh the "sentimental romanticism" about "little human beings in the early stages of pregnancy."[63]

---

[61] Ibid., 410.

[62] Means, "Phoenix of Abortional Freedom," 403. Means cited this passage as reprinted in Thomas Cooper, *Tracts on Medical Jurisprudence* (Philadelphia, 1819). Though Means notes rightly that the early common law proscribed abortion after "quickening" (i.e., detection of fetal movement), it also should be noted that Means did not confine his views to the early stages of pregnancy. The fetus did not become a person deserving legal protection, Means argued, until a certain degree of cortical development occurred at around nine months of gestation. See ibid., 409.

[63] Ibid., 403–04.

Means' assertion that there was *no better evidence* of the framers' view of abortion as a common-law liberty than Samuel Farr's medical treatise was, however, either deliberately dishonest or grossly negligent. Dr. Farr's reference to the embryo as a "monster" occurred within a technical discussion of deformed and disabled adults (whom he also referred to as "monsters") and the phrase "human creature," in this context, signified the form rather than the species of the being in question. When, just a few pages later, Farr did consider the question of when human life begins, he answered unequivocally "immediately after conception," and he argued against some of his own colleagues who posited erroneously (a) that life begins only after quickening; (b) that life begins after the seventh, fourteenth, or thirtieth day after conception; or (c) that "a foetus, as long as it continues in the womb, where it does not breath, cannot be called a living animal." Removing all possible ambiguity from his position, Farr even insisted that "life must certainly begin after conception, and nothing but the arbitrary forms of human institutions can make it otherwise"[64] and

> that abortions, or the destruction of those unborn embryos which were never brought into the world: and indeed as such beings might live, and become of use to mankind, and as they may be supposed indeed from the time of conception, to be living animated beings, there is no doubt but the destruction of them ought to be considered a capital crime.[65]

As it turns out, Dr. Farr's estimate of the wrong of abortion and the moral worth of the embryo resembled the very "sentimental romanticism" of which Means opined, and, according to Means' own methodology, gave striking evidence that the general culture in 1787 considered abortion to be a grave and serious injustice.[66]

---

[64] Samuel Farr, *Elements of Medical Jurisprudence*, 2nd ed. (London, 1814), 23–24.
[65] Ibid., 69–70.
[66] In the same book that Means cites as an authority for eighteenth-century abortion law, physician George Male notes that abortion after quickening was a capital offense in English statutory law after 1803 and indicates his

As Cyril Means was laying the scholarly groundwork for his new abortion history, it was evident to anyone who had looked into the historical record that Means' research was deeply flawed. David Tundermann, a Yale Law student working with Norma McCorvey's legal team during his summer break in 1971, wrote an internal memorandum to this effect, noting that Means' "own conclusions sometimes strain credibility." Still, echoing a sentiment that has animated the way some scholars and jurists have approached abortion history, Tundermann nonetheless concluded that

> Where the important thing to do is to win the case no matter how, however, I suppose I agree with Means's technique: begin with a scholarly attempt at historical research; if it doesn't work out, fudge it as necessary; write a piece so long that others will read only your introduction and conclusion; then keep citing it until the courts begin picking it up. This preserves the guise of impartial scholarship while advancing the proper ideological goals.[67]

Although aware of the serious flaws in Means' historical research, Sarah Weddington nonetheless thought it "important to note" in oral arguments that

> in a law review article recently submitted to the Court and distributed among counsel by Professor Cyril Means, Jr., entitled "The Phoenix of Abortional Freedom," that at the time the Constitution was adopted there was no common law prohibition against abortions; that they were available to the women of this country.[68]

Starting from the faulty premise that abortion was a common-law liberty, Weddington then tied her argument together by insisting that the right to abortion was protected

own position that it is "probable that the foetus is animated at the moment of conception, and the crime committed then is morally as great as at any other period of pregnancy." Thomas Cooper, *Tracts on Medical Jurisprudence* (Philadelphia, 1819), 206. Cf. Statutes at Large, 43 Geo. III, ch. 28.

[67] Memo from David Tundermann to Roy Lucas, "Legislative Purpose et al.," 5 August 1971, cited in David Garrow, *Liberty and Sexuality*, 891–892, n. 41.

[68] Oral argument in *Roe v. Wade* (13 December 1971), http://www.oyez.org/cases/1970-1979/1971/1971_70_18/.

by the Fourteenth Amendment under the "rights of persons to life, liberty, and the pursuit of happiness."[69] Perhaps an unintentional slip, Weddington's echo of the words of the Declaration of Independence at this point in her argument – rather than the words of the Fourteenth Amendment – brings the issue full circle to the unavoidable moral and philosophical nexus between *Dred Scott* and *Roe v. Wade*. The meaning and significance of the assertion in the Declaration of Independence that "all men are created equal" and "endowed by their Creator with certain inalienable rights" – and its relevance to American constitutionalism – was at the heart of the debate over the decision in *Dred Scott*, and it has become central to the debate over abortion. The temptation of many opponents of the Court's *Roe* decision has been to criticize any substantive interpretation of the Fourteenth Amendment – including, or perhaps *especially*, an interpretation that is grounded in a theory of natural rights – as contrary to the text, logic, and structure of the Constitution. But this dismissal of substantive due process on originalist grounds disregards the complexity of the nineteenth-century debate over the Due Process Clause and the inevitability of substantive moral reasoning in constitutional interpretation. One example of this nearsightedness is the frequent omission of the fact that the *Dred Scott* dissenters rested their opinions, in part, on the unenumerated premise that slavery is against

---

[69] Ibid. For an overview of the status of abortion at common law, see, generally, Joseph Dellapenna, *Dispelling the Myths of Abortion History*, supra n. 48. See also William Blackstone, *Commentaries on the Laws of England: in Four Books* (Philadelphia: R. Welsh, 1902–1915), Vol. 1, 117–18. Blackstone describes life as a "right inherent by nature in every individual" that "begins in contemplation of law as soon as an infant is able to stir in the mother's womb," and he categorizes abortion as a "very heinous misdemeanor" at common law. Cf. James Wilson, "Lectures on Law" (1790–1791), in Kermit L. Hall and Mark David Hall, eds., *The Collected Works of James Wilson*, 2 vols. (Indianapolis: Liberty Fund, 2007), Vol. 2, 1068: "With consistency, beautiful and undeviating, human life, from its commencement to its close, is protected by the common law. In the contemplation of the law, life begins when the infant is first able to stir in the womb. By the law, life is protected not only from immediate destruction, but from every degree of actual violence, and, in some cases, from every degree of danger."

natural law and therefore a matter of local municipal law only.
The question of whether Dred Scott was a citizen entitled to
sue in federal court depended on the answer to the antecedent
question of whether he was made free by his residence in free
jurisdictions, and the dissenters, as well as Lincoln and the
Republicans, appealed to well-established precedents, running
back to *Somerset v. Stewart* (1772), to claim that "slavery was
so repugnant . . . nothing could be suffered to support it but
positive law."[70]

The importance and relevance of the moral status of slavery to the *Dred Scott* case is precisely why Abraham Lincoln
made the Declaration of Independence the centerpiece of his
rhetorical attack on the Court's decision. The real issue in
*Dred Scott*, Lincoln repeatedly declared, was whether slavery
was wrong, and he knew his political opponents could not
defend the moral propriety of slavery without first denying,
or at least distorting, the principles of the Declaration.
And, indeed, those "Jeffersonian axioms," Lincoln recalled,
were, in his day, "denied and evaded, with no small show of
success. One dashingly calls them 'glittering generalities';
another bluntly calls them 'self-evident lies'; and still others
insidiously argue that they apply only to 'superior races.'"[71]
The real point of disagreement, then, sprung from a "difference of sentiment – the belief on the part of one that the
institution [of slavery] is wrong . . . and this other sentiment,
that it is no wrong."[72]

Similarly, the question lingering at the heart of *Roe* is
whether there is anything about human nature that is relevant to the moral worth and status of human beings as such.
For if human beings at every stage of development had been
recognized as rights-bearers in some fundamental moral
sense, then it would have strained credulity to insist
that the Fourteenth Amendment, written to secure the

---

[70] *Somerset v. Stewart* 1 Lofft 17, 19 (1772).

[71] Roy P. Basler, ed., *Collected Works of Abraham Lincoln*, 8 vols. (New Brunswick, NJ: Rutgers University Press, 1953), Vol. 3, 375.

[72] Ibid., Vol. 3, 226.

fundamental rights of human nature to all persons, prohibited states from protecting one class of human beings
from the private use of lethal force. The oral arguments in
*Roe* demonstrate the awareness of the justices that this was
indeed the initial hurdle. As Justice Stewart suggested to
Weddington's agreement, without a constitutionally relevant moral distinction between a human being before and
after birth, the proclaimed liberty interest in abortion would
logically allow a mother who "thought that it bothered her
health having a child around" to "have it killed."[73] The
outcome in *Roe* thus depended on the premise defended by
Cyril Means that "prior to birth, the offspring of human
parents" is not a "human *person*," and that the framers of
the Constitution "thought that 'person' does not include a
foetus, but does include the newborn babe."[74]

## THE SUBSTANCE OF *ROE*

*Roe* posited a sharp dichotomy between born persons and
unborn non-persons for the purposes of constitutional
interpretation, and partisans of the decision have been
quick to point out that defining "constitutional persons"
simply as individual members of the human species would
have been "more radical than even the most ardent
opponents of *Roe* appear to realize."[75] As Ronald
Dworkin insists, "If a fetus is a constitutional person,
then states not only *may* forbid abortion but in some
circumstances *must* do so."[76] Because the Due Process
Clause proscribes only state action ("no state shall"), the
practical consequences would likely come to bear on the
Fourteenth Amendment's Equal Protection Clause. "The
important effect of personhood under equal protection,"

---

[73] Oral reargument in *Roe v. Wade* (11 October 1972), http://www.oyez.org/
cases/1970-1979/1971/1971_70_18/reargument.
[74] Cyril Means, "The Phoenix of Abortional Freedom," 409.
[75] Ian Shapiro, ed., *Abortion: The Supreme Court Decisions, 1965–2007*, 3rd ed.
(Indianapolis, IN: Hackett Publishing Company, 2007), xv.
[76] Dworkin, *Life's Dominion* (New York: Knopf, 1993), 110.

Gerard Bradley explains, "would be inclusion of the unborn within the protection of state homicide statutes that proscribe various ways of 'causing the death of another person.'"[77]

As it is, our political culture is conflicted about how best to characterize the wrong of third-party fetal homicide (i.e., whether it is a harm to the woman only or also to the unborn child), and state laws currently embody inconsistent principles with respect to the protection of the unborn under homicide statutes.[78] Until there is some resolution of the issue in the general political culture, the legal doctrine that unborn human beings are constitutional persons under the Fourteenth Amendment (with its potentially radical consequences) will "never be more than a curiosity."[79] Given the state of American society today, it also is not obvious that the complexities surrounding the law as it concerns the unborn child can or should be resolved by the federal judiciary. Judges and politicians who would return the question of abortion to the states therefore seek a *modus vivendi* that is both prudent and pragmatic. But regardless of the political authority tasked with resolving this issue – state legislatures, Congress, or the courts – abortion implicates deep questions that are unavoidably bound up with basic constitutional commitments. Far from resolving these issues, the Supreme Court's forty-year foray into abortion politics has only heightened them. In particular, the Court's dual assertion in *Roe* (a) that unborn human beings are constitutional non-persons and (b) that the Constitution prohibits states from protecting unborn human beings from destruction in some circumstances bring to the fray a

---

[77] Gerard Bradley, "*Life's Dominion*: A Review Essay," *Notre Dame Law Review* 69, no. 2 (1993–94), 344–45.

[78] For a general discussion of personhood and state fetal homicide statutes, see Jean Reith Schroedel, *Is the Fetus a Person? A Comparison of Policies across the Fifty States* (Ithaca, NY: Cornell University Press, 2000).

[79] Robert Bork, "Constitutional Persons: An Exchange on Abortion," *First Things* (January 2003). Reprinted in *Human Life Review* (Winter 2003), 28.

set of constitutional questions rooted in the logic of republicanism and the separation of government powers.

A related consequence of *Roe*, as is often noted, was the creation of a vibrant national anti-abortion movement not unlike the anti-slavery movement of the 1850s. As Robert George (a scholar and endogenous participant in the anti-abortion movement) argues,

> When it comes to cases such as *Dred Scott* and *Roe*, there seem to be but two options available to citizens who recognize the profound injustice these decisions work: either citizens are to treat the legitimacy of the Constitution as gravely weakened, or they are to deny that the Court has the authority to settle definitively the meaning of the Constitution – in other words, either the Constitution is illegitimate or the Court is behaving illegitimately.[80]

For many of the Republicans opposed to the *Dred Scott* decision, the chosen solution was to maintain fidelity to the Constitution but deny that the Supreme Court is the final arbiter of constitutional meaning. While abiding by the outcome of the decision in *Dred Scott* with respect to the parties involved in the suit, Republicans publicly challenged the Supreme Court's interpretation of the Constitution and insisted that the logic of constitutional government precluded the Court from binding the co-ordinate branches of government in future policy making.

On the floor of the House of Representatives, Rep. John Bingham (R-OH) expounded the logic of this position:

> If the Supreme Court is to decide all constitutional questions for us, why not refer every question of constitutional power to that body not already decided, before acting upon it. I recognize the decisions of that tribunal as of binding force only as to the parties and privies to the suit, and the rights particularly involved and passed upon. The court has no power in deciding the right of Dred Scott and of his children to their liberty, to decide, so as to bind this body, that neither Congress, nor a Territorial Legislature, nor any human

---

[80] Robert George, "Justice, Legitimacy, and Allegiance: 'The End of Democracy?' Symposium Revisited" in Sotirios A. Barber and Robert P. George, eds., *Constitutional Politics: Essays on Constitution Making, Maintenance, and Change* (Princeton, NJ: Princeton University Press, 2001), 323–24.

power, has authority to prohibit slavery in the Territories; neither has that tribunal power to decide that five million persons, born and domiciled in this land, "have no rights which we are bound to respect."[81]

Abraham Lincoln, as well, took this tack in his opposition to the *Dred Scott* ruling. As the Supreme Court had declared Dred Scott to be a slave, Lincoln insisted, he would not attempt through private force to make him free. At the same time, Lincoln declared that the other branches of government were not bound to follow the principles of the Court's decision as a "political rule,"[82] and, in his First Inaugural Address, Lincoln argued that if "the policy of the Government upon vital questions is to be irrevocably fixed by the Supreme Court," then the "people will have ceased to be their own rulers, having to that extent practically resigned their government into the hands of that eminent tribunal."[83]

Still, Republicans did not fault the Supreme Court for reviewing the *Dred Scott* case, since, as Lincoln insisted, deciding the rights of parties in cases properly brought before the Court is a duty from which the justices "may not shrink."[84] Neither did they ground their opposition to the Court's opinion in an amoral or non-substantive view of the Fifth Amendment's Due Process Clause, which would allow the legislature to take any property, destroy any life, or restrain any liberty, provided that it was done under the auspices of generally agreed upon legal procedures. Rather, they insisted, along with John Bingham, that due process of law meant "law in its highest sense, that law which is the perfection of human reason, and which is impartial, equal, exact justice."[85] This, of course, did not mean that slavery was constitutionally abolished everywhere in the United

---

[81] Rep. John Bingham (R-OH), 36th Congress, 1st session (24 April 1860), H. 1839.
[82] Basler, ed., *Collected Works of Abraham Lincoln*, Vol. 2, 495 and Vol. 3, 255.
[83] Ibid., Vol. 4, 268.
[84] Ibid.
[85] Rep. John Bingham (R-OH), *Congressional Globe*, 39th Congress, 1st session (28 February 1866), H. 1094.

States when the Fifth Amendment was adopted (despite the obvious ways in which persons were being deprived of liberty without due process), as such a reading of the Constitution would have been practically implausible given the entrenchment of slavery in society.[86]

Similarly, it is theoretically possible to read the Fourteenth Amendment as *requiring* states to prohibit abortion. Whatever theoretical merit such a view has, however, those advocating it today – like the radical anti-slavery constitutionalists of the nineteenth century – are not making legal arguments likely to win a case but rather are engaging in critical normative theorizing. Yet even at this level, the slavery controversy works as a heuristic device to illuminate the current debate about abortion. Deep questions involving personhood, natural rights, republicanism, and self-government are all present (with the added complexity of American federalism after the passage of the Fourteenth Amendment) and those searching for historical analogs of *Roe v. Wade* may indeed find a lesson in the history of the *Dred Scott* case. The proper analogy, however, is not to be found in the common denunciation of a moral reading of the Constitution as inherently problematic. Rather, the nexus penetrates deeper to the principles underlying the constitutional order, and we would do well to engage these moral issues rather than dismiss them as somehow peripheral to the persistent *Dred Scott/Roe* analogy. Over the last forty years – with developments in both medicine and law – the new constitutional questions implicated by *Roe* have only served to underscore the impossibility of avoiding such substantive constitutional analysis.

---

[86] Such a reading was theoretically possible. See, e.g., Lysander Spooner, *The Unconstitutionality of Slavery* (Boston: 1860).

# 4

# Constitutional Disharmony after *Roe*

As the late Samuel Huntington noted in his seminal work on American political development, "an ever-present gap exists between American political ideals and American political institutions and practice."[1] If we understand a constitution as the fundamental norms, principles, and practices of a particular society (including the scheme of distributing political power), we might characterize the gap or tension between ideals and practice as a kind of constitutional disharmony. In the American context, Huntington argued, such disharmony has been particularly acute because of the "central role of moral passion" in American politics, which has given rise to myriad reform movements that appeal to foundational moral principles such as those prominently featured in the preamble to the Declaration of Independence.[2] The classic example of disharmony, along these lines, was occasioned by the institution of slavery, which created convulsions in the polity precisely because slavery was inconsistent with the normative principles underlying the regime.

As Jennifer Hochschild writes, the American system of race-based, hereditary chattel slavery was "antiliberal in its

---

[1] Samuel P. Huntington, *American Politics: The Promise of Disharmony* (Cambridge, MA: Harvard University Press, 1981), 4.
[2] Ibid., 11.

assertion of the unequal worth of persons, of civil – not natural – determinations of rights, of the legitimacy of denying liberty and opportunity to some."[3] Of course, scholars still debate the best way to conceptualize the relationship between slavery and the principles of American government. One answer to the question of how slavery could co-exist with a political culture that emphasized liberty and individual rights is that slavery was simply an aberration. Another possible explanation, however, is that rights-oriented liberalism and racial slavery were actually symbiotic. A version of the symbiosis argument was prominently put forward by Edmund Morgan in his study of slavery in eighteenth-century Virginia.[4] What made freedom and equality among the Virginia elites possible was the relative equality of leisure and economic resources provided by the system of forced labor. Liberal ideology among whites flourished, in other words, precisely because slavery was endemic to the system. This was, in fact, one of the justifications of slavery offered by Southerners who considered slavery to be a positive good for white society.[5] To put this another way: A liberalism of natural rights could be practically reconciled with slavery only so long as slaves were considered foreign to the moral community of persons. This practical reconciliation required an artificial distinction between rights-bearing moral persons and all others, but the violence inherent in the system of chattel slavery made such an artificial distinction difficult to maintain over time.

---

[3] Jennifer Hochschild, *The New American Dilemma: School Desegregation and Liberal Democracy* (New Haven, CT: Yale University Press, 1984), 2. Scholars operating under this assumption include classical twentieth-century interpreters Myrdal and Hartz. See Gunnar Myrdal, *An American Dilemma: The Negro Problem and American Democracy* (New York: Harper and Row, 1944), and Louis Hartz, *The Liberal Tradition in America* (New York: Harcourt, 1955).

[4] See Edmund S. Morgan, *American Slavery, American Freedom: The Ordeal of Colonial Virginia* (New York: W. W. Norton, 1975).

[5] See generally David F. Ericson, *The Debate Over Slavery: Antislavery and Proslavery Liberalism in Antebellum America* (New York: New York University Press, 2000).

The nuances in the debate about how best to conceptualize the relationship between slavery and American ideals map directly onto the current debate about abortion. Both sides in the abortion debate appeal to elements of what Huntington succinctly called the American Creed – "liberal, individualistic, democratic, egalitarian."[6] Defenders of abortion choice emphasize the centrality of abortion to the maintenance of equal rights and opportunities for women, while critics of abortion emphasize the equal rights of all human beings, including the unborn. Ostensibly peering beyond the liberal veneer of their opponents, partisans on the respective sides of the abortion debate allege either that the rhetoric of preserving fetal life is bound up with a desire to preserve illiberal and inegalitarian gender roles[7] or that the rhetoric of abortion choice belies a deep illiberal and inegalitarian prejudice against the unborn.[8] Conflict over abortion has thus centered, to a large degree, on the meaning and application of the egalitarian principles underlying the American regime.

And yet, like the violence accompanying the system of slavery, the violence inherent in abortion cannot ultimately be reconciled with American liberalism. Indeed, the true extent of the constitutional disharmony manifest by the practice of abortion has unfolded gradually in the decades after *Roe*. "The tendency of a principle to expand itself to the limit of its logic," Benjamin Cardozo once observed, "may be counteracted by the tendency to confine itself

---

[6] Huntington, *American Politics*, 4.

[7] See, e.g., Reva Siegel, "Abortion," in Richard Weightman Fox and James T. Kloppenberg, eds., *Companion to American Thought* (Oxford: Blackwell Publishers, 1995), 2, and "Brief for 281 Historians as Amici Curiae in Support of Appellees" in *Webster v. Reproductive Health Services* 492 U.S. 490 (1989) (1989 U.S. S. Ct. Briefs LEXIS 1525).

[8] See, e.g., Gerard V. Bradley, "Life's Dominion: A Review Essay," *Notre Dame Law Review* 69 (1993–1994), 329–391, and John Finnis, remarks delivered at the conference "Open Hearts, Open Minds, and Fair-Minded Words," *Princeton University*, October 15–16, 2010. Reprinted in John Finnis, "The Other F-Word," *The Public Discourse: Ethics, Law, and the Common Good* (October 20, 2010), http://www.thepublicdiscourse.com/2010/10/1849.

within the limits of its history."[9] The history undergirding
Justice Blackmun's opinion in *Roe*, however, could not confine the constitutional novelty of the right to abortion. Once
the unborn were deemed to be constitutional non-persons,
and abortion held to be a fundamental right, there was
nothing in principle to obstruct the full logical outgrowth
of the abortion liberty. Although Blackmun originally
insisted that the right to abortion was not "unqualified,"
and Chief Justice Burger emphasized that the Constitution
did not protect "abortions on demand," the relevant question
after 1973 was, why not?[10]

## THE LOGIC OF THE ABORTION LIBERTY

Although the constitutional right to abortion announced by
the Court in *Roe* flowed naturally from the history constructed by key figures in the abortion reform movement,
it was, in reality, deeply incongruous with the traditional
criminal and civil laws of the various states and, indeed,
with the deeper principles at the heart of American constitutionalism. While the case was still working its way
through the federal court system, a research note in the
*Notre Dame Lawyer* tersely summarized the collateral
effects of the constitutional attacks on criminal abortion
statutes: "The result ... has been further confusion in an
already inconsistent area of the law – the law with respect to
the unborn child."[11] As late as 1964, a prominent law
professor could declare, without controversy, that

> [M]edical authority has recognized long since that the child is in
> existence from the moment of conception, and for many purposes
> its existence is recognized by the law. The criminal law regards it as
> a separate entity, and the law of property considers it in being for

[9] Benjamin N. Cardozo, *The Nature of the Judicial Process* (Mineola, NY: Dover, 2005), 41.
[10] *Roe* v. *Wade* 410 U.S. 113, 154 (1973) (Blackmun, J.); *Doe* v. *Bolton* 410 U.S. 179, 180 (1973) (Burger, J., concurring).
[11] William L. Maledon, "The Law and the Unborn Child: The Legal and Logical Inconsistencies," *Notre Dame Lawyer* 46 (1971), 349–372.

all purposes which are to its benefit, such as taking by will or descent. ... All writers who have discussed the problem have joined ... in maintaining that the unborn child in the path of an automobile is as much a person in the street as the mother.[12]

Constitutional attacks on state abortion laws, however, threw the legal status of the unborn child into question. If this being was, in the eyes of the law, a non-person whom the state could not protect through criminal abortion statutes, what became of the status of the unborn child in other areas of criminal and civil law? And, on a deeper level, what did *Roe* implicitly presume to be the general foundation of individual rights in the constitutional order?

At a minimum, the logic of Justice Blackmun's opinion seemed to regard human status as *irrelevant* to the question of who may claim rights under the Constitution. Blackmun even went so far as to insist the Court "need not resolve the difficult question of when life begins."[13] As John Noonan noted, Blackmun's dismissal of the question of life's origins implicitly assumed a positivist jurisprudence whereby a person is "no natural reality but a construction of juristic thinking."[14] In the annals of American history, the best (and perhaps only) parallel example of such an explicit disregard for basic humanity in the construction of legal personhood was the law governing slavery.

Of course, as a practical matter, the presumption that a slave was a non-person could never entirely take hold in American law. As Madison insisted in *Federalist* no. 54, the law regarded slaves both as property *and* as persons. By nature, they could not entirely take on the characteristics of chattel, and the law, by protecting the slave

---

[12] W. Prosser, *Handbook of the Law of Torts* §56, 355, 3rd ed. (1964). Cited in *Notre Dame Lawyer* 46 (1970–71), 349–50.

[13] *Roe* v. *Wade*, 159 (Blackmun, J.).

[14] John T. Noonan, *A Private Choice: Abortion in America in the Seventies* (New York: Free Press, 1979), 13–14. See Hans Kelsen, *The Pure Theory of the Law* (Berkeley: University of California Press, 1967), 95.

in his life and limbs, against the violence of all others, even the
master of his labor and his liberty; and in being punishable himself
for all violence committed against others – the slave is no less
evidently regarded by the law as a member of the society, not as a
part of the irrational creation; as a moral person, not as a mere
article of property.[15]

There was a deep tension, however, in the various ways
in which slaves were regarded within the American constitutional order, and constitutional theorists have long highlighted the discord between slavery and the underlying
principles of the American regime. "Slavery in the United
States," Gary Jacobsohn argues, "may have produced a
body of settled law, but its incompatibility with the precepts
of constitutionalism rendered its status as a constitutionally
sanctioned inheritance fatally suspect."[16] There was an
inherent disharmony between the fundamental principles
of American constitutionalism – legitimate authority based
on the consent of the governed, limitations on arbitrary
executive power, natural rights by virtue of a common
humanity – and the institution of chattel slavery.

The reason slavery created such normative problems in
the constitutional order is precisely because the law treated
human beings, in certain fundamental respects, as property
rather than persons. Many of the founders saw this problem
clearly. At the Constitutional Convention, Madison insisted
that it would be "wrong to admit in the Constitution
the idea that there could be property in men" because
men, by nature, were not consumable merchandise.[17]
Opponents of the Constitution, as well, drew attention to
the disharmony between slavery and the underlying principles of a republican government. The convention delegate
turned anti-Federalist Luther Martin took issue with the
Constitution precisely because it hedged, in various ways,

---

[15] Clinton Rossiter, ed., *The Federalist Papers* (New York: Penguin, 2003), 334.

[16] Gary Jeffrey Jacobsohn, "Constitutional Identity," *The Review of Politics* 68
(2006), 375.

[17] Max Farrand, ed., *The Records of the Federal Convention of 1787*, 3 vols.
(New Haven, CT: Yale University Press, 1911), Vol. 2, 417 (August 25, 1787).

"the *only branch* of *commerce* which is *unjustifiable in its nature,* and *contrary* to the *rights* of *mankind.* . . . *[S]lavery,*" Martin insisted, "is *inconsistent* with the *genius* of *republicanism,* and has a tendency to *destroy* those *principles* on which it is *supported,* as *it lessens the sense* of the *equal rights* of *mankind,* and habituates us to *tyranny* and *oppression.*"[18] Although the Constitution referred to slaves only as "persons," it did accommodate state institutions and practices that reduced some human beings to the impersonal status of property. Legal personhood in the original constitutional order did not fully correspond to the community of natural persons (composed, by definition, of all human beings).

A similar understanding of personhood is implicit in Blackmun's exegetical approach to the Fourteenth Amendment. Although the Nixon appointee recognized that the "Constitution does not define 'person' in so many words," he assumed that it had a legal meaning that could be constructed independent of its natural meaning.[19] In a legal brief, Blackmun noted, the state of Texas had laid out "at length and in detail the well known facts of fetal development."[20] Drawing from medical journals and embryology textbooks, Texas maintained that "modern science – embryology, fetology, genetics, perinatology, all of biology – establishes the humanity of the unborn child."[21] The scientific evidence was uncontroversial and fairly straightforward:

> From conception the child is a complex, dynamic, rapidly growing organism. By a natural and continuous process the single fertilized ovum will, over approximately nine months, develop into the trillions of cells of the newborn. The natural end of the sperm and ovum is death unless fertilization occurs. At fertilization a new and

---

[18] Ibid., Vol. 3, 211–12 (November 29, 1787).
[19] *Roe* v. *Wade,* 157 (Blackmun, J.).
[20] Ibid., 157.
[21] Brief for Appellee, *Roe* v. *Wade* (*U.S. Supreme Court Records and Briefs, 1832–1978,* Gale/Cengage Learning Document Number: DW100136546), 31.

unique being is created which, although receiving one-half of its chromosomes from each parent, is really unlike either.[22]

For Blackmun, however, those facts were not dispositive of the question of whether the unborn child was a *constitutional* person. Because other references to the word "person" in the Constitution – such as the qualifications for senators and representatives – had no "antenatal application," and because of Blackmun's (mistaken) insistence that abortion was historically a common-law liberty, he asserted that the "word 'person,' as used in the Fourteenth Amendment does not include the unborn."[23]

Still, Blackmun outlined his own preliminary caveats to the abortion liberty in the latter half of his *Roe* opinion. Although the unborn were not constitutional persons, and either the Ninth Amendment or the Fourteenth Amendment (or perhaps both) protected the right to abortion, states could constitutionally enact restrictions during later stages of pregnancy.[24] After the first three months of gestation, Blackmun declared, states were permitted to craft regulations designed to promote maternal health, and after fetal viability (i.e., the point at which the baby could theoretically survive outside of the womb), the state could, "if it chooses, regulate, and even proscribe, abortion except where it is necessary, in appropriate medical judgment, for the preservation of the life or health of the mother."[25] In a companion

---

[22] Ibid., 32. The brief cited the following sources: Alex Ingleman-Sunderberg and Cloes Wirsen, *A Child is Born: The Drama of Life Before Birth* (New York: Dell, 1965); Leslie B. Arey, *Developmental Anatomy*, 6th ed. (Philadelphia: W. B. Saunders, 1954); Bradley M. Patten, *Human Embryology*, 3rd ed. (New York: McGraw-Hill, 1968). For an accessible summary of the facts established by modern embryology, see Robert P. George and Christopher Tollefsen, *Embryo: A Defense of Human Life* (New York: Doubleday, 2008), 27–56.

[23] *Roe v. Wade*, 158 (Blackmun, J.).

[24] Ibid., 153: "The right of privacy, whether it be founded in the Fourteenth Amendment's concept of personal liberty and restrictions upon state action, as we feel it is, or, as the District Court determined, in the Ninth Amendment's reservation of rights to the people, is broad enough to encompass a woman's decision whether or not to terminate her pregnancy."

[25] Ibid., 164–165.

case to *Roe* decided the same day, Blackmun further clarified that "health," in this context, was something to be
determined by "medical judgment ... exercised in the light
of all factors – physical, emotional, psychological, familial,
and the woman's age – relevant to the wellbeing of the
patient."[26]

In practical terms, the Court's decision boiled down to
this: State legislatures could constitutionally proscribe abortion only after fetal viability, but such a categorical ban
would not extend to any abortion deemed by the presiding
physician to be necessary for his or her patient's well being,
broadly understood. Still, even within this framework,
there were questions. Could states mandate particular abortion methods over others,[27] require parental or spousal
consent,[28] require physicians to determine whether the
fetus is viable before performing an abortion,[29] impose a
twenty-four-hour waiting period,[30] or require the presence
of a second physician for post-viability abortions?[31] For
nearly two decades, the Court gave a negative answer to
each of these questions.

When the occasion arose to revisit *Roe* in *Planned
Parenthood* v. *Casey* (1992), however, the judicial land-
scape had been dramatically altered by a series of
Court appointments under Presidents Reagan and Bush.

[26] *Doe* v. *Bolton*, 192 (Blackmun, J.).
[27] *Planned Parenthood* v. *Danforth* 428 U.S. 52 (1976) (declaring unconstitutional a Missouri law requiring a physician to perform an abortion with the
method most likely to preserve the life of the fetus).
[28] Ibid. (holding a Missouri spousal consent law and parts of a parental consent
law unconstitutional).
[29] *Franklin* v. *Colautti* 439 U.S. 379 (1979) (holding void for vagueness a section
of the 1974 Pennsylvania Abortion Control Act requiring physicians to determine fetal viability before performing an abortion).
[30] *City of Akron* v. *Akron Center for Reproductive Health* 462 U.S. 416 (1983)
(holding, in part, that mandating a twenty-four-hour waiting period before
performing an abortion does not serve a legitimate state interest).
[31] *Thornburgh* v. *American College of Obstetricians and Gynecologists* 476 U.S.
747 (1986) (holding, in part, that a section of the 1982 Pennsylvania Abortion
Control Act requiring the presence of a second physician for post-viability
abortions does not serve a legitimate state interest).

Republican nominees O'Connor, Scalia, Kennedy, Thomas, and Souter now sat on the Court alongside *Roe*'s original dissenters, Rehnquist and White. The new conservative tilt of the Court led many observers to sound the death knell of *Roe v. Wade*, but such announcements proved to be premature. Immediately at issue in *Casey* were several amendments to the Pennsylvania Abortion Control Act, which, among other things, required a woman to give informed consent to an abortion procedure, instituted a twenty-four-hour waiting period, mandated parental consent for minors and spousal notification for married women, and imposed reporting requirements on any abortion facility operating within the commonwealth.[32]

Although the Court ultimately upheld all but the spousal notification requirement, *Casey* was, at most, a Pyrrhic victory for *Roe*'s detractors. In a plurality opinion authored by three Republican appointees, the Court reaffirmed what it deemed to be "*Roe*'s central holding":

> First is a recognition of the right of the woman to choose to have an abortion before viability and to obtain it without undue interference from the State. Before viability, the State's interests are not strong enough to support a prohibition of abortion or the imposition of a substantial obstacle to the woman's effective right to elect the procedure. Second is a confirmation of the State's power to restrict abortions after fetal viability, if the law contains exceptions for pregnancies which endanger a woman's life or health. And third is the principle that the State has legitimate interests from the outset of the pregnancy in protecting the health of the woman and the life of the fetus that may become a child.[33]

For all of the public turmoil surrounding the announcement of the Court's decision, the situation on the ground remained essentially unchanged. Subject to regulations that were not unduly burdensome, women in all fifty states were at liberty to obtain abortions at any stage of pregnancy, provided the

---

[32] Pennsylvania Abortion Control Act of 1982, §§3205–3214.
[33] *Planned Parenthood v. Casey* 505 U.S. 833, 846 (1992) (O'Connor, Kennedy, and Souter, JJ.).

abortion was, in the opinion of their attending physician, necessary to protect their life or health.

## "PARTIAL-BIRTH" ABORTION
## AND THE LOGIC OF *ROE*

After reaffirming the central holding in *Roe*, the *Casey* plurality invited the contending sides in the abortion controversy to "end their national division by accepting a common mandate rooted in the Constitution."[34] In a turn of events that diminished even the slim chances of obtaining such a constitutional truce, a new abortion technique soon captured the public's attention and further polarized the nation. Just a few months after *Casey*, Dr. Martin Haskell delivered a controversial paper at the National Abortion Federation Risk Management Seminar describing a procedure that was designed to minimize some of the complications and health risks associated with second- and third-trimester abortions. The new procedure was a variation of a common abortion method known as dilation and evacuation (D&E), which involves the dismemberment of a developing fetus inside a woman's uterus. One of the risks associated with this method is that the boney fragments of the dismembered fetus will damage the woman's uterus or vagina as the doctor attempts to recover and evacuate the dismembered body parts. To minimize this risk, Dr. Haskell began using a technique that "differs from classical D&E in that it does not rely upon dismemberment to remove the fetus."[35] In a procedure he called dilation and extraction (D&X), the fetus is instead left "intact" and delivered

---

[34] Ibid., 867.
[35] Martin Haskell, M.D., "Dilation and Extraction for Late Second Trimester Abortion," Presented at the National Abortion Federation Risk Management Seminar, September 13, 1992. The paper specified that the procedure was used on twenty- to twenty-six-week-old fetuses; still, Dr. Haskell acknowledged that at least one other physician used a similar technique "up to 32 weeks or more" and that his technique "can be used in the third trimester."

breach into the vaginal canal. "At this point," Dr. Haskell explained,

> the right-handed surgeon slides the fingers of the left hand along the back of the fetus and "hooks" the shoulders of the fetus with the index and ring fingers (palm down). Next he slides the tip of the middle finger along the spine towards the skull while applying traction to the shoulders and lower extremities . . .
>
> While maintaining this tension, lifting the cervix and applying traction to the shoulders with the fingers of the left hand, the surgeon takes a pair of blunt curved Metzenbaum scissors in the right hand. He carefully advances the tip, curved down, along the spine and under his middle finger until he feels it contact the base of the skull under the tip of his middle finger.
>
> Reassessing proper placement of the closed scissors tip and safe elevation of the cervix, the surgeon then forces the scissors into the base of the skull or into the foramen magnum. Having safely entered the skull, he spreads the scissors to enlarge the opening.
>
> The surgeon removes the scissors and introduces a suction catheter into this hole and evacuates the skull contents. With the catheter still in place, he applies traction to the fetus, removing it completely from the patient.[36]

One of Dr. Haskell's nurses offered this less clinical description of the D&X procedure to the Senate Judiciary Committee, which Justice Kennedy later had occasion to note:

> Dr. Haskell went in with forceps and grabbed the baby's legs and pulled them down into the birth canal. Then he delivered the baby's body and the arms – everything but the head. The doctor kept the head right inside the uterus . . .
>
> The baby's little fingers were clasping and unclasping, and his little feet were kicking. Then the doctor stuck the scissors in the back of his head, and the baby's arms jerked out, like a startle reaction, like a flinch, like a baby does when he thinks he is going to fall.
>
> The doctor opened up the scissors, stuck a high-powered suction tube into the opening, and sucked the baby's brains out. Now the baby went completely limp . . .
>
> He cut the umbilical cord and delivered the placenta. He threw the baby in a pan, along with the placenta and the instruments he had just used.[37]

---

[36] Ibid.
[37] *Gonzales v. Carhart* 550 U.S. 124, 139 (2007) (Kennedy, J.).

For Americans with ordinary sensibilities, the details of this new procedure were jarring, to say the least, and they seemed to call into question, yet again, the true meaning and legacy of the principle laid down in *Roe*. Almost immediately after the *Casey* decision, battles on the legislative front centered on proposed bans of the D&X procedure, which became known, in the popular lexicon, as "partial-birth" abortion. A Republican-controlled Congress, nominally acting under its power to regulate interstate commerce, soon passed legislation to criminalize any "abortion in which the person performing the abortion partially vaginally delivers a living fetus before killing the fetus and completing the delivery."[38] Although Congress was unable to muster the votes necessary to override President Clinton's veto, bans of almost identical wording proliferated at the state level. One such example was a Nebraska statute prohibiting any "abortion procedure in which the person performing the abortion partially delivers vaginally a living unborn child before killing the unborn child and completing the delivery."[39] For clarification, the statute described the criminal act as "deliberately and intentionally delivering into the vagina a living unborn child, or a substantial portion thereof, for the purpose of performing a procedure that the person performing such procedure knows will kill the unborn child and does kill the unborn child."[40] While allowing an exception to the law in situations where, in the doctor's medical judgment, the "physical life" of the woman would be threatened, neither the congressional ban nor the Nebraska statute contained a corresponding health exception.

In a legal challenge with national implications, Dr. Leroy Carhart alleged that Nebraska's statute was inconsistent with the principles underlying *Roe* and *Casey*, and, in *Stenberg* v. *Carhart* (2000), five members of the Court

---

[38] Partial-Birth Abortion Ban Act (1995), H.R. 1833.
[39] Nebraska Rev. Stat. Ann Sec. 28–328. See *Stenberg* v. *Carhart* 530 U.S. 914, 922 (2000) (Breyer, J.).
[40] Ibid.

agreed. "First, the law lacks any exception 'for the preservation of the ... health of the mother,'" Justice Breyer explained, citing the Court's prior decision in *Casey*. "Second, it 'imposes an undue burden, on a woman's ability' to choose a D&E abortion, thereby unduly burdening the right to choose abortion itself."[41] Carhart had alleged, not implausibly, that this ban on partial-birth abortion could be construed to prohibit other abortions where a live fetus passes through the cervix into the vagina before being killed. In a standard D&E procedure, it was not uncommon, for example, for the doctor to use the friction between the fetus and the cervix to "disarticulate" the fetus's body. While it was not his intention to deliver the fetus "intact" during a standard D&E procedure, Dr. Carhart testified in a federal district court that dismemberment of the fetus does often occur after a "substantial portion" of the "living unborn child" (as the Nebraska statute is worded) has already passed into the birth canal. The likely result, according to Justice Breyer, was that "some present prosecutors and future Attorneys General may choose to pursue physicians who use D&E procedures."[42] Such a result, the Court declared, could not pass constitutional scrutiny.

## THE LINE BETWEEN ABORTION AND INFANTICIDE

It was a serious question, then, in light of the Court's ruling, whether a state could even protect a child during the process of birth. What constituted being "born" for constitutional purposes, and when did "constitutional personhood" begin? When a substantial portion of the child's body was outside of the cervix? Once the child was completely separate from the body of the mother? These were serious questions that were not easily dismissed. When *Roe* v. *Wade* was decided in 1973, the state of Texas had on its books a

---

[41] *Stenberg* v. *Carhart*, 930 (Breyer, J.).
[42] Ibid., 945.

statute that would, if challenged today, inevitably bring within its orbit discussions of partial-birth abortion.

Though the D&X procedure did not exist as an accepted medical practice, Texas' criminal abortion code did provide:

> Whoever shall during parturition of the mother destroy the vitality or life in a child in a state of being born before actual birth, which child would otherwise have been born alive, shall be confined in the penitentiary for life or for not less than five years.[43]

During oral arguments in 1972, Thurgood Marshall asked Texas Attorney General Robert Flowers to clarify the meaning of the parturition statute, which led to the following exchange:

> JUSTICE MARSHALL: What does that statute mean?
> MR. FLOWERS: Sir?
> JUSTICE MARSHALL: What does it mean?
> MR. FLOWERS: I would think that –
> JUSTICE STEWART: That it is an offense to kill a child in the process of childbirth?
> MR. FLOWERS: Yes sir. It would be immediately before childbirth, or right in the proximity of the child being born.
> JUSTICE MARSHALL: Which is not an abortion.
> MR. FLOWERS: Which is not – would not be an abortion, yes, sir. You're correct, sir. It would be homicide.[44]

The comments of Justices Marshall and Stewart seemed to indicate that the deliberate killing of a child during the process of childbirth would be a species of homicide rather than constitutionally protected abortion, but the line separating the two could not be so easily drawn after thirty years of legal and technological developments. Once it reached the outer limits of its logic, the principle undergirding *Roe* seemed to protect abortion by any method at any stage of gestation prior to full completion of live birth, albeit

---

[43] Texas Rev. Civ. Stat. Art. 4512.5. The statute was the only part of the criminal abortion code to survive the legal challenge in *Roe*, and it remains part of Texas' state law. See http://www.statutes.legis.state.tx.us/Docs/CV/pdf/CV.71.6-1_2.pdf.

[44] Oral reargument in *Roe* v. *Wade* (11 October 1972), http://www.oyez.org/cases/1970-1979/1971/1971_70_18/reargument.

with some non-burdensome state regulations. After the decisions in *Casey* and *Stenberg*, our law, in other words, had come quite close to embodying the principle urged by the original appellant in *Roe*: "that the woman's right is absolute and that she is entitled to terminate her pregnancy at whatever time, in whatever way, and for whatever reason she alone chooses."[45]

*Roe*'s opponents, embattled after the *Stenberg* decision, decided to turn their attention to what Hadley Arkes – the principal architect of the federal Born-Alive Infants Protection Act – had described, years earlier, as a "modest first step": the legal protection of a child that was inadvertently born alive during an attempted abortion procedure. The strategy was clearly one calculated to provoke public debate and reflection about the scope and logic of the abortion liberty. What made the prospect of legislatively protecting the lives of children born during failed abortion procedures "more than a thought-experiment," Arkes explained,

> was *Floyd* v. *Anders*, a case that arose in a federal district court in South Carolina in 1977. A male child had survived an abortion, and the question was posed to whether there had been an obligation to preserve the life of that child. The answer, tendered by Judge Clement Haynsworth, was no: As Haysworth "explained," the mother had decided on abortion, and therefore "the fetus in this case was not a person whose life state law could protect." Ordinarily, a child born alive is protected under the laws of a state, but now we had a new constitutional right, a right to abortion, and that new right worked its effects simply by shifting the labels: That child born alive was not a child, or a person, protected by the laws of homicide.[46]

The problem, highlighted by *Floyd* v. *Anders*, was that the difference in mere inches between being born and unborn was essentially arbitrary. That fact could lead in one of two directions. On the one hand, children in the process of birth

---

[45] *Roe* v. *Wade*, 153 (Blackmun, J.).
[46] Hadley Arkes, *Natural Rights and the Right to Choose* (New York: Cambridge University Press, 2002), 95.

could – as Marshall, Stewart, and Flowers seemed to indicate during oral arguments in *Roe* – be protected under state laws against homicide, for at this point the act of abortion seems to be much closer to traditionally accepted definitions of infanticide. On the other hand, the argument could be made that killing a child immediately after birth is not any different, as a matter of principle, than killing a child during birth, and such logic might persuade some that parents ought to be able to maintain discretion over the lives of even born children.[47]

This precisely was the defense put forward in the mid-1980s by a Texas doctor who was charged with homicide after he "performed an abortion by hysterectomy in which the fetus was withdrawn alive" and then intentionally suffocated, submerged in a bucket of water, and sealed in a plastic bag.[48] A jury found that the doctor did "intentionally and knowingly cause the death of an individual" contrary to the state's criminal code, and, accordingly, the doctor was sentenced to fifteen years in prison. On appeal, attorneys for the defendant insisted that the infant girl delivered alive by hysterectomy was, according to the Supreme Court's jurisprudence, "a non-individual" left unprotected by the criminal prohibition against homicide. Though a Texas appeals court sustained the doctor's conviction, other prominent examples of live birth abortion came to light across the country, and a fundamental question – apparently left unsettled by *Roe* – was brought to the public's attention: Did a right to abortion include a right to kill or "abort" a child after she was born?[49]

---

[47] Contemporary arguments in defense of infanticide are treated in more detail in Chapter 7.

[48] *Showery* v. *Texas* 690 S.W.2d 689, 691 (1985) (Ward, J.).

[49] For congressional testimony regarding the practice of so-called live birth abortion, see *Born-Alive Infants Protection Act: Hearings on H.R. 2175 Before the Subcommittee on the Constitution of the House Committee on the Judiciary*, 107th Cong., 1st Sess., July 12, 2001 (statement of Jill L. Stanek, R.N.); *Born-Alive Infants Protection Act: Hearings on H.R. 4292 Before the Subcommittee on the Constitution of the House Committee on the Judiciary*, 106th Cong., 2nd Sess., July 20, 2000 (statement of Allison Baker, R.N., B.S.N.).

The strategy of putting forward legislation to protect infants born alive during botched abortion procedures put proponents of legal abortion in an awkward position. While no public official would readily go on record as supporting a right to infanticide, the effort to protect children previously marked for abortion had a clear pedagogical purpose, for "to explain why the child bears an intrinsic dignity" worthy of legal protection, Arkes suggested, was "to put in place the premises that would finally undercut, or dissolve, the 'right to abortion' and all of the jurisprudence built upon that slogan."[50] When he was still an Illinois State Senator, Barack Obama tried to navigate this pro-life trap by protesting against the logic of a bill that would "fully recognize as a human person"[51] a baby born alive during an attempted abortion. What worried Obama was that legally protecting "a fetus or child – as some might describe it" that was "still temporarily alive outside the womb" would be tantamount to saying that "they are persons entitled to the kinds of protections that would be provided to a – a child, a nine month old – child that was delivered to term."[52] As a Harvard-trained lawyer, Obama immediately perceived the danger this principle posed to the abortion regime built upon *Roe*. When the bill came up again the following year, Obama declared flatly (and presciently) that the "issue ultimately is about abortion and not live births."[53]

Although the various "Born Alive" bills proposed in Illinois were effectively killed in committee, pro-life organizations had greater success at the national level. Just a few months after Obama voiced his misgivings about the proposed Illinois statute, Congress passed a law providing that "the words 'person', 'human being', 'child', and 'individual'" in any Act

---

[50] Arkes, *Natural Rights and the Right to Choose*, 95.

[51] Sen. O'Malley, 92nd General Assembly, Illinois State Senate Transcript (March 30, 2001).

[52] Sen. Obama, 92nd General Assembly, Illinois State Senate Transcript (March 30, 2001).

[53] Sen. Obama, 92nd General Assembly, Illinois State Senate Transcript (April 4, 2002).

of Congress or administrative regulation "shall include every infant member of the species homo sapiens who is born alive at any stage of development."[54] With that premise firmly planted in the law, pro-life organizations then sought to revisit the issue of partial-birth abortion. In November of 2003, Congress passed a national Partial-Birth Abortion Ban Act similar to the bill vetoed by Clinton nearly a decade earlier. This time, however, Congress went to great lengths to describe the procedure in a way that would not inadvertently sweep other abortion procedures within its purview. Partial-birth abortion, as it was defined in the 2003 statute, was

> an abortion in which a physician deliberately and intentionally vaginally delivers a live, unborn child's body until either the entire baby's head is outside the body of the mother, or any part of the baby's trunk past the navel is outside the body of the mother and only the head remains inside the womb, for the purpose of performing an overt act (usually the puncturing of the back of the child's skull and removing the baby's brains) that the person knows will kill the partially delivered infant, performs this act, and then completes the delivery of the dead infant.[55]

Confident that its description did not suffer for vagueness, Congress then asserted, based on its own factual findings, that such a procedure was never medically necessary to preserve the health of a pregnant woman.

Dr. Carhart immediately initiated a legal challenge directed at the national statute, and the resulting case was argued at the bar of the Supreme Court in November 2006. The *Stenberg* decision seemed to be almost exactly on point against the congressional ban, but the replacement of Sandra Day O'Connor with Samuel Alito upset the Court's previous balance. With this change of personnel in place, some observers hoped, while others feared, that the Court would, for the first time since 1973, uphold an outright ban on a particular type of abortion procedure. Thus, when oral arguments began in *Gonzales* v. *Carhart*, tensions were high,

---

54 Born-Alive Infants Protection Act (2002), 116 Stat. 976.
55 Partial-Birth Abortion Ban Act (2003), 18 U.S.C. 1531.

and the presumed stakes extended far beyond the particular procedure – applicable only to a small fraction of all abortions – that was the subject of the federal statute.

## THE OUTER EDGES OF THE ABORTION LIBERTY

Much of the ground covered in *Gonzales* had been well trod by the competing parties in *Stenberg*. The *amicus curiae* briefs, the oral arguments, even the questions by the justices, all seemed to be round two of the same fight. Whereas the government insisted that the "basic point of this statute is to draw a bright line" between abortion and infanticide,[56] opponents of the ban maintained, as they had in *Stenberg*, that the description of "partial-birth abortion" in the bill would likely be construed to include common dilation and extraction (D&E) abortions as well. In a standard D&E procedure, Dr. Carhart's counsel pointed out, the relevant facts sometimes fit the description of partial-birth abortion. Although it is common in a D&E

> for the physician to dismember the fetus due to the traction caused by pressure at the cervix, physicians may also bring the fetus out largely intact. At that point the physician may either dismember the fetus, or, if the entire fetus but for the head has been removed, take steps to reduce the size of the skull, or take other steps in order to remove the fetus as safely as possible. . . . If the fetus is still living, any of these actions will inevitably cause fetal demise.[57]

Additionally, as Dr. Carhart pointed out, such an intact delivery was arguably *safer* for the woman, because it did not require dismemberment of the fetus (thus reducing both the number of instrument passes into the uterus and the likelihood that sharp fetal bone fragments would damage the woman's internal organs during "evacuation" of fetal body parts).

---

[56] Oral argument in *Stenberg* v. *Carhart* (25 April 2000), http://www.oyez.org/cases/1990-1999/1999/1999_99_830/argument.

[57] "Brief of National Abortion Federation, et al., as Amici Curiae in Support of Respondant," *Gonzales* v. *Carhart* (2006) (2006 U.S. S. Ct. Briefs LEXIS 656, 27).

Opponents of the Partial-Birth Abortion Ban Act also drew attention to the fact that many abortions were susceptible to descriptions equally as gruesome as that of so-called partial-birth abortion. The grisly nature of *all* abortions in the second and third trimesters, it was suggested, made the prohibition of *any* abortion for reasons of decency essentially arbitrary. As Justice Ginsburg asserted, citing Stevens' *Stenberg* opinion: "the notion that either of these two equally gruesome procedures [i.e., D&E and D&X] ... is more akin to infanticide than the other, or that the State furthers any legitimate interest by banning one but not the other, is simply irrational."[58] But if it was indeed irrational to distinguish between the killing of a baby whose "body past the trunk is outside the body of the mother" and the killing of a baby still *in utero*, it was surely just as irrational to make a further distinction for a baby already born – since the point of Ginsburg's argument was that the location of the baby during his or her death was irrelevant.

Drawing out this point, Justice Scalia asked during oral arguments whether "it would be lawful or would it be infanticide to deliver the fetus entirely and just let it expire without any attempt to keep it alive?"[59] If keeping a baby intact were sometimes safer for the mother than dismembering him or her in the womb, then surely a live birth, in some instances, would be the *safest* option on the table. If that were the case – if the considered medical judgment of the attending physician was that the baby should be delivered alive and then killed (or allowed to die) – would this not also be a protected method of abortion? It was an uncomfortable question to ask, but it seemed to flow logically from the

58 *Gonzales* v. *Carhart*, 182 (Ginsburg, J. dissenting).
59 Oral argument in *Gonzales* v. *Carhart* (8 November 2006), http://www.oyez.org/cases/2000-2009/2006/2006_05_380/opinion. Or, as Roberts asked: "And in giving your arguments toward the safety benefits of the D&X, I couldn't understand why they wouldn't also apply to the total delivery of the fetus in the vertex delivery situation [in which the skull has already passed the cervix]. . . . In other words, if you want as much of the fetus intact and out as possible, why wait, stop it halfway?" Ibid.

argument. In response to Scalia's query, Solicitor-General Paul Clement insisted to the contrary that "if somebody tried to, with the fetus, you know, perfectly alive and in the hours that it might have to live, if somebody came in and ripped its head open, I think we'd call that murder."[60] Ginsburg quickly cut off that line of questioning, insisting that "anything about infanticide, babies, all that, is just beside the point."[61] But, of course, in a very real way it *wasn't* beside the point, for one of Ginsburg's own arguments against the ban was that "it doesn't preserve any fetus because you just do [the abortion] inside the womb instead of outside."[62] Which only begs the question: When an abortion is performed "outside the womb," is that or is it not infanticide? Only by tautologically defining abortion as something different than "infanticide, babies, all that" could the question of the legal status of a partially born child be deemed irrelevant to the case at hand.

For many, it was a surreal place to which we had traveled in the thirty-four years between *Roe* and *Gonzales*. In 1973, many states, including Texas, had statutes on the books (most in effect since the mid-nineteenth century) that prohibited any abortion that was unnecessary to save the life of the mother. By the turn of the twenty-first century, the national debate had moved to the question of whether legislatures could prohibit abortions when part of the baby was already outside of the mother's body. The logic of the abortion liberty had traveled to its outer limits, and serious challenges, when they came, came only at the margins. During the debates on the Partial-Birth Abortion Ban Act, however, there was an unavoidable confrontation with some of the more uncomfortable questions left unsettled in *Roe*, including the question of *what* was being destroyed in these surgeries.

[60] Ibid.
[61] Ibid.
[62] Ibid.

Originally, the Court had feigned a position of neutrality on the question of whether abortion ended a life. "When those trained in the respective disciplines of medicine, philosophy, and theology are unable to arrive at any consensus, the judiciary," Justice Blackmun asserted, "at this point in the development of man's knowledge, is not in a position to speculate as to the answer."[63] Similar agnosticism about life has led to confused positions by some of abortion's most ardent supporters, such as Sen. Barbara Boxer (D-CA), who maintained during congressional debates on partial-birth abortion that she "didn't believe in killing any human being."[64] When asked by Sen. Rick Santorum (R-PA) when a child was protected by the Constitution, Boxer nonetheless answered:

> I would make this statement: The Constitution, as it currently is – some of you want to amend it to say life begins at conception. I think that when you bring your baby home, when your baby is born – and there is no such thing as partial-birth – the baby belongs to your family and has all the rights.[65]

A human being, according to Boxer's working definition, was only a human being if it was born *and* wanted by her family. And abortion, by tautology, was not the killing of a human being.

In *Gonzales*, however, no one had room to speculate as to whether the object of abortion was human. The majority opinion contained stomach-churning descriptions of abortion methods, noting various ways in which a living baby's skull is punctured and its brain removed during D&X procedures. Sometimes, Justice Kennedy noted, the fetus is killed "a day or two" before the procedure by an injection of digoxin or potassium chloride, a drug, he pointed out, that was also used in state executions. In his description of the more common D&E procedure, which was unquestionably

---

[63] *Roe* v. *Wade*, 159 (Blackmun, J.).
[64] *Congressional Record*, 106th Cong., 1st Sess., S. 12878–12880 (20 October 1999).
[65] Ibid.

constitutional according to ruling Supreme Court precedent, Kennedy detailed, as well, how

> The doctor, often guided by ultrasound, inserts grasping forceps
> through the woman's cervix and into the uterus to grab the fetus.
> The doctor grips a fetal part with the forceps and pulls it back
> through the cervix and the vagina, continuing to pull even after
> meeting resistance from the cervix. The friction causes the fetus to
> tear apart. For example, a leg might be ripped off the fetus as it is
> pulled through the cervix and out of the woman. The process of
> evacuating the fetus piece by piece continues until it has been
> completely removed. A doctor may make 10 to 15 passes with
> the forceps to evacuate the fetus in its entirety, though sometimes
> removal is completed with fewer passes. Once the fetus has
> been evacuated, the placenta and any remaining fetal material are
> suctioned or scraped out of the uterus. The doctor examines the
> different parts to ensure the entire fetal body has been removed.[66]

Kennedy also cut through the circumlocutions typical of
the abortion controversy by using "unborn child," "baby,"
"infant," and "fetus" interchangeably throughout the opinion.

The dissenters took issue with such language, complain-
ing that it evidenced the "Court's hostility to the right *Roe*
and *Casey* secured."[67] And of course it did. The full logic of
the right pronounced in *Roe* depended, for consistency, on a
distinction between unborn children, who may be destroyed
at will, and persons, who are the subjects of constitutional
rights against arbitrary violence (or, at a minimum, the
equal protection of state homicide statutes). The only way
for the right in *Roe* to make sense as a human right was
to place the unborn outside of the community of rights-
bearing human beings. As it has become more and more
difficult to sustain Blackmun's facile assertion that it is
merely "potential" life at stake in these surgeries, it has
therefore become necessary to defend what honest observers
can only describe as killing. The discussions in *Stenberg*
and *Gonzales* did, after all, center on "fetal demise"
(i.e., death) and the various methods by which it could be

---

[66] *Stenberg* v. *Carhart*, 135–136 (Kennedy, J.).
[67] *Gonzales* v. *Carhart*, 186 (Ginsburg, J. dissenting).

procured. And it is precisely the right to determine when and how to cause fetal demise that abortion supporters see as central to "a woman's autonomy to determine her life's course, and thus to enjoy equal citizenship stature."[68] As Ginsburg asserted in her *Gonzales* dissent, anything that calls the scope of that right into question, such as legislative bans on partial-birth abortion, "cannot be understood as anything other than an effort to chip away at a right declared again and again by this Court – and with increasing comprehension of its centrality to women's lives."[69]

## ABORTION, HISTORY, AND THE FOURTEENTH AMENDMENT

Still, many of the most committed defenders of abortion rights were at least squeamish about defending *this* kind of abortion procedure, and, as David Smolin provocatively suggested in an essay for the *Harvard Journal of Law & Public Policy*, some of the justices' willing acquiescence in the inherent brutality of late-term abortions found a striking historical parallel with the institution of slavery.[70] Faced with the fact that slavery was a legally protected institution, antebellum judges often confronted questions involving the scope or logic of the right of a master over his slave. Did a legal right to the services of a slave also imply a right to use whatever means necessary to force the slave to render those services? Or, to ask the question from a different angle, could the legislature protect the slave against some forms of gratuitous violence, even if that violence came by the hand of the one to whom he owed labor? These questions highlighted a tension implicit in the law of slavery, and that tension was difficult to maintain over time. To fit within the

---

[68] Ibid., 173.
[69] Ibid., 191.
[70] David Smolin, "Fourteenth Amendment Unenumerated Rights Jurisprudence: An Essay in Response to *Stenberg* v. *Carhart*," *Harvard Journal of Law & Public Policy* 24, no. 3 (2001) 815–839.

larger constitutional order, bound up, as it was, with the
ideas of equality and natural rights, the institution of slavery
seemed to require the complete dehumanization of the slave
and the full divestiture of the slave's legal personhood.
In the paradigmatic North Carolina case of *State* v.
*Mann* (1829),[71] Judge Thomas Ruffin – later hailed by Roscoe
Pound as one of the "great judges of the formative era of
our law" – drew out what he took to be the logical conclusion of the right to slavery.[72] Though Ruffin acknowledged that there was a struggle in his "own breast between
the feelings of the man, and the duty of the magistrate," he
steeled his nerves enough to trace the implications of the
right in question. In the case before him, a slave girl named
Lydia had been hired out to a third party, who proceeded to
"chastise her" for "some small offence" before shooting her
in the back as she ran away.[73] A North Carolina jury had
found the defendant's actions "cruel and unwarrantable,
and disproportionate to the offence committed by the
slave."[74] Upon appeal, Judge Ruffin, for the state's highest
court, asserted that assault on a slave "by a hirer" was not
an indictable offense, for

> The end [of slavery] is the profit of the master, his security and the
> public safety; the subject, one doomed in his own person, and his
> posterity, to live without knowledge, and without the capacity to
> make any thing his own, and to toil that another may reap the
> fruits. What moral considerations shall be addressed to such a
> being, to convince him what, it is impossible but that the most
> stupid must feel and know can never be true – that he is thus to
> labour upon a principle of natural duty, or for the sake of his
> personal happiness, such services can only be expected from one
> who has no will of his own; who surrenders his will in implicit
> obedience to that of another. Such obedience is the consequence
> only of uncontrolled authority over the body. There is nothing else
> which can operate to produce the effect. The power of the master

---

[71]  *State* v. *Mann* 13 N.C. 263 (1829).
[72]  Roscoe Pound, *The Formative Era of American Law* (Boston: Little, Brown &
      Co., 1938), 84.
[73]  *State* v. *Mann*, 263 (Ruffin, J.).
[74]  Ibid.

must be absolute, to render the submission of the slave perfect. I most freely confess my sense of the harshness of this proposition, I feel it as deeply as any man can. And as a principle of moral right, every person in his retirement must repudiate it. But in the actual condition of things, it must be so. There is no remedy. This discipline belongs to the state of slavery. They cannot be disunited, without abrogating at once the rights of the master, and absolving the slave from his subjection ... it is inherent in the relation of master and slave.[75]

As Smolin notes, "Justice Ruffin therefore did not merely lament that slavery was built upon uncontrolled authority over the slave but instead pushed the law further in that brutal direction." The Court's similarly steely-eyed embrace of the brutality inherent in both the D&E and D&X procedures, Smolin further suggests, makes *Stenberg* v. *Carhart* the "*State* v. *Mann* of abortion jurisprudence."[76]

As it was with the legal right to slavery, the private use of force is inseparable from the legal right to abortion. As Ruffin acknowledged, the state generally prohibited assault "immoderately inflicted by a private person," but "with slavery it is far otherwise." The institution of slavery could not exist if the private use of force by the master was not preserved *in toto*. The "wrath of a master" against his slave, Ruffin noted, was "generally practiced with impunity, by reason of its privacy."[77] In the abortion debates, as well, "privacy" has become the catchword, delineating a realm of activity (including the use of force necessary to procure "fetal demise") that the state is powerless to proscribe. Of course, the uncomfortable implications of this aspect of the abortion liberty can be lessened by abstractions and euphemisms, notably the classification of the unborn as something less than human. And yet such abstractions are difficult to honestly maintain in the cases in which a D&E or D&X procedure would be appropriate, for there is just no way to describe the procedure without acknowledging that human

---

[75] Ibid., 266–67.
[76] Smolin, "Fourteenth Amendment Unenumerated Rights Jurisprudence," 832.
[77] *State* v. *Mann*, 267 (Ruffin, J.).

bones are breaking and parts of a human body are being dismembered and evacuated by the doctor.

In defending a private right to abortion under the Constitution, Justice Blackmun did not engage these difficult questions about what or whom was the object of the abortion procedure, instead laying great emphasis on the history of abortion in America. "Our task," Blackmun asserted,

> of course, is to resolve the issue by constitutional measurement, free of emotion and of predilection. We seek earnestly to do this, and, because we do, we have inquired into, and in this opinion place some emphasis upon, medical and medical-legal history and what that history reveals about man's attitudes toward the abortion procedure over the centuries.[78]

That history was largely fabricated for ideological reasons, and the Court's abortion jurisprudence, in the years since *Roe*, has become increasingly disconnected from any historical moorings. Nowhere is this more apparent than the Court's near total neglect of the history of the Fourteenth Amendment and, in particular, its immediate historical context in the long and tortuous struggle over the institution of slavery. It is noteworthy, as well, that critics of the Court's abortion decisions, beginning in *Roe* and continuing through *Stenberg*, have steadfastly compared them to the Court's most notorious slavery ruling, *Dred Scott v. Sandford* (1857), which required the Fourteenth Amendment to overturn its stunted constitutional interpretation. If anything has remained constant in the forty years after *Roe*, it is the ubiquitous sense, among many conscientious citizens, that on some level of deep principle, the abortion controversy is a reenactment of a battle already fought and a betrayal of rights already won.

A key to understanding some of the ideological developments that led to this shift in constitutional principle can be found in an editorial published in a 1970 issue of *California*

---

[78] *Roe* v. *Wade*, 116 (Blackmun, J.).

*Medicine.* The article, which was *supportive* of the "clearly changing attitudes toward human abortion" among the elite classes in society, framed the contemporary conflict over abortion as one between the "traditional Western ethic" that had long emphasized "the intrinsic worth and equal value of every human life regardless of its stage or condition" and a new social ethic of "relative rather than absolute values on such things as human lives." Because the old ethic had "not yet been fully displaced in society it had been necessary [for the purposes of reform] to separate the idea of abortion from the idea of killing." Giving an accurate description of the disharmonic interplay between the old ethic and the new, the editorial went on:

> The result has been a curious avoidance of the scientific fact, which everyone really knows, that human life begins at conception and is continuous whether intra- or extra-uterine until death. The very considerable semantic gymnastics which are required to rationalize abortion as anything but taking a human life would be ludicrous if they were not often put forth under socially impeccable auspices. It is suggested that this schizophrenic sort of subterfuge is necessary because while a new ethic is being accepted the old one has not yet been rejected.[79]

Today, the situation is little changed. The conflict between the liberal norms and principles that continue to hold sway over a large segment of society are at odds with the social practice of abortion, and the conflict leads many abortion rights advocates to characterize abortion as something other than the killing of a human being. With partial-birth abortion, this way out of cognitive dissonance is difficult to maintain, however, because the debate is centered on particular methods of procuring "fetal demise" that require jurists and policy makers to engage in detailed discussions of abortion techniques. Like the institution of slavery, the violence inherent in the practice of abortion manifests a deep constitutional disharmony that will be resolved only with

[79] "A New Ethic for Medicine and Society," *California Medicine: The Western Journal of Medicine* 113, no. 3 (1970), 67–68.

the abandonment (or radical reinterpretation) of our liberal principles or the recovery of the traditional idea, long at the base of "most of our laws and much of our social policy" that every human life has an "intrinsic worth and equal value."[80] Of course, the amendment to the Constitution designed to remedy the wrongs of slavery was precisely the amendment seized by the Court, more than a century later, to promulgate a general right to abortion. A question, then – part historical and part philosophical – lingers: How did we get here?

---

[80] Ibid., 67.

# 5

# The Politics of Abortion History

Shortly after Norma McCorvey filed her lawsuit against the Dallas District Attorney, inaugurating what would become the landmark case of *Roe* v. *Wade* (1973), a similar case was docketed for the Northern District Court of Ohio. In *Steinberg* v. *Brown* (1970), a pregnant twenty-one-year-old welfare recipient with a dependent child at home and an estranged husband (along with a physician, a psychiatrist, a social worker, and a minister) initiated a class action lawsuit challenging the constitutionality of Ohio's long-standing abortion ban. "No person," the Ohio Revised Code stipulated, "shall prescribe or administer a medicine, drug, or substance, or use an instrument or other means with intent to procure the miscarriage of a woman unless such miscarriage is necessary to preserve her life, or is advised by two physicians to be necessary for that purpose."[1] In this case, a three-judge federal court was asked to declare Ohio's anti-abortion statute unconstitutional. The right to privacy protected by various provisions in the Bill of Rights and made applicable against the states by the Fourteenth Amendment, it was argued, protected the right of Ohio women to seek and obtain abortions free from state legislative interference.

[1] Ohio Revised Code, Sec. 2901.16 (1970).

Yet a bill to revise and strengthen the restrictive abortion law at issue in *Steinberg* had been passed by the Ohio state legislature on April 16, 1867 – just four months after the same legislature had voted to ratify the Fourteenth Amendment.[2] Similar abortion laws existed in state codes throughout the country when Secretary of State William Seward certified that the required 3/4 of state legislatures had also voted for ratification. Those same abortion statutes had remained on the books, largely unchanged, until the legal challenges of the 1970s. For jurists and scholars adhering to traditional canons of constitutional interpretation, an obvious question emerged: How could a statutory regime in place in 1868 and left undisturbed for over a century be deemed unconstitutional?[3]

In an attempt to meet this challenge, the general historical narrative that was developed by advocates of abortion reform was twofold. First, they suggested that the primary reason for nineteenth-century state abortion laws (like the Ohio statute in question) was to protect women from dangerous surgeries and abortifacient drugs and *not* to protect or safeguard the lives of unborn children (whom, it was claimed, were always considered to be non-persons by the law). Second, legal reformers insisted that abortion was a traditional common law liberty in England and America. Because advances in medical technology had made abortion relatively safe for women, it was urged that judicial decisions striking down these century-old laws would fulfill the spirit of the original statutes (i.e., to protect women) while maintaining an essential continuity with the Anglo-American constitutional tradition. This

---

[2] See *General and Local Laws and Joint Resolutions of the State of Ohio* (Columbus, OH: L. D. Meyers & Bro., 1867), Vol. 64, 202–3.

[3] As James Stoner notes, "[I]n a rule of interpretation typical of the classical common law, it is presumed that a constitutional provision that at the time of its adoption apparently left undisturbed an existing common law or statutory regime cannot be invoked to destroy it." See James Stoner, "Common Law and Constitutionalism in the Abortion Case," *Review of Politics* 55, no. 3 (1993), 436–7.

narrative, in turn, provided the foundation for the decision in *Roe* v. *Wade*.

The reasons that historically had been advanced to justify state abortion restrictions, Justice Blackmun asserted in *Roe*, were to (a) discourage illicit sex, (b) regulate a medical procedure that was inherently dangerous for women, and (c) protect prenatal life. According to Blackmun, however, the first concern was anachronistic and "no court or commentator [had] taken the argument seriously"; the second was rendered moot because of advances in medical technology that made abortion safer for women; and the third was "sharply disputed" owing to an alleged "absence of legislative history."[4] Appealing to two of New York Law School Professor Cyril Means' academic articles, Blackmun even noted that there was "some scholarly support" for the view that the "original purpose" of the state anti-abortion statutes was solely to protect women.[5]

While serving as legal counsel to the National Association for the Repeal of Abortion Laws (NARAL), Means wrote his legislative history of abortion statutes with the stated goal of providing judges a historical foundation for a new constitutional abortion regime. As Means readily admitted, the notion that the unborn child was "itself an object of protection by our criminal law" was a "common assumption" in 1968. In an article for the *New York Law Forum*, however, Means purported to reveal "for the first time" that the true purpose of state anti-abortion statutes was *only* to protect the life and health of the mother.[6] In a companion article published three years later, Means summarized his "original contribution":

> [T]he revelation of a truth that had been long forgotten: that the sole historically demonstrable legislative purpose behind these

---

[4] *Roe* v. *Wade* 410 U.S. 113, 147–153 (1973) (Blackmun, J.).
[5] Ibid., 113, 152.
[6] Cyril C. Means, Jr., "The Law of New York Concerning Abortion and the Status of the Foetus, 1664–1968: A Case of Cessation of Constitutionality," *New York Law Forum* 14, no. 3 (1968) 411–515.

statutes was the protection of pregnant women from the danger to their lives imposed by surgical or portional abortion, under medical conditions then obtaining, that was at times as great as the risk to their lives posed by childbirth at term, and that concern for the life of the conceptus was foreign to the secular thinking of the Protestant legislators who passed these laws.[7]

In his second article, Means claimed to have uncovered a related "story, untold now for nearly a century" that "English and American women enjoyed a common-law liberty to terminate at will an unwanted pregnancy, from the reign of Edward III to that of George III" and this "common-law liberty endured ... in America, from 1607 to 1830."[8] The upshot of Means' history was clear enough. Speaking of the Georgia case of *Doe* v. *Bolton* and the Texas case of *Roe* v. *Wade* (which were both scheduled for oral argument at the Supreme Court) Means concluded: "Should the merits be reached in either case, counsel and the Court may find the present conspectus of the Anglo-American legal history of abortion of assistance; for, only if in 1791 elective abortion was a common-law liberty, can it be a ninth-amendment right today."[9]

The problem was that Means' two central claims about the history of abortion law were simply not true. No court in England or America ever considered abortion (even if unindictable) to be a protected common-law liberty, and the primary purpose of anti-abortion legislation was unequivocally to protect the lives of unborn children, who were considered to be both human beings and legal persons by the doctors who proposed and lobbied for, and the legislators who passed, restrictive abortion statutes in the mid-nineteenth century. As Ken Kersch notes in a different context, many of the constitutional theorists and

---

[7] Cyril C. Means, Jr., "The Phoenix of Abortional Freedom: Is a Penumbral Right or Ninth Amendment Right About to Rise from the Nineteenth-Century Legislative Ashes of a Fourteenth-Century Common-Law Liberty?" *New York Law Forum* 17, no. 2 (1971) 335–36.

[8] Means, "The Phoenix of Abortional Freedom," 336.

[9] Ibid.

legal historians who created "constitutional narratives of
the trajectory of twentieth-century constitutional development" were "endogenous and invested participants in
this process."[10] As one such endogenous participant in
the abortion reform movement, Cyril Means fashioned a
linear constitutional narrative to provide a historical foundation for constitutional abortion rights.

The two main tenets of Means' narrative – that abortion
was a common-law liberty at the time of the American
founding and that the sole purpose of nineteenth-century
anti-abortion statutes was the protection of women – have
helped to sustain the current abortion regime by purporting
to connect it with America's constitutional past. A good
example of this continued effort to connect post-*Roe* abortion jurisprudence to America's past social practices is in
an *amicus* brief signed by 281 historians and submitted to
the Supreme Court for the case of *Webster* v. *Reproductive
Health Services* (1989). After insisting that "constitutional
principles require examination of our history and tradition
as a Nation to determine the existence and contours of
fundamental constitutional rights," the *Historians' Brief*
repeated Means' twin claims that "nineteenth-century laws
restricting access to abortion were not based on a belief that
the fetus is a human being" and that "the common law
recognized a woman's right to choose abortion."[11] The
*Historians' Brief*, in turn, has informed some of the most
influential scholarship on jurisprudence and constitutional
law, including the works of such prominent scholars as
Ronald Dworkin and Laurence Tribe,[12] and a shared

[10] Ken I. Kersch, *Constructing Civil Liberties; Discontinuities in the
Development of American Constitutional Law* (Cambridge University
Press, 2004), 360.

[11] "Brief for 281 Historians as Amici Curiae in Support of Appellees," *Webster* v.
*Reproductive Health Services* 492 U.S. 490 (1989) (1989 U.S. S. Ct. Briefs
LEXIS 1525, 44 and 48). Hereafter *Historians' Brief*.

[12] See, for example, Laurence Tribe, *The Clash of Absolutes* (New York: W. W.
Norton, 1990), 28–29, 258 n. 1, and Ronald Dworkin, *Life's Dominion*
(New York: Knopf, 1993), 111–112, 249 n. 8.

commitment to this false narrative about America's history and traditions has been an important aspect of the creation and maintenance of constitutional abortion rights.

## MEANS, MOHR, AND THE PHOENIX OF ABORTION FREEDOM

"In ancient Eastern folklore," Means recounted in 1971, "the phoenix was a fabulous bird, said to live for five hundred years in the Arabian desert, then to build its own funeral pyre, on which it would burn itself to ashes, out of which it would then arise young again."[13] In anticipation of the Court's decision in *Roe*, Professor Means suggested that the life of the abortion liberty in America might soon come to resemble that of the mythical phoenix. In the early days of the Republic, Means argued, "American women enjoyed a common-law liberty to terminate at will an unwanted pregnancy," but the traditional liberty to abort had been reduced to ashes by restrictive abortion laws passed in the mid-nineteenth century.[14] There were, however, new challenges to state abortion laws afoot in the courts, and Means offered his "legal history of abortion" to assist "counsel and the Court" in their deliberations.[15]

When the cases were heard, counsel and the Court did indeed take notice. The Justices reportedly had copies of Means' article with them on the bench, *Roe*'s attorney Sarah Weddington appealed to Means's history as authoritative during oral arguments, and Blackmun cited Means seven times in his official opinion for the Court.[16] Additionally, nearly half of Blackmun's opinion involved an inquiry into "medical and medical-legal history," and the Court's decision rested, in part, on the premise that in

---

[13] Means, "The Phoenix of Abortional Freedom," 335.
[14] Ibid., 336.
[15] Ibid.
[16] *Roe v. Wade*, n. 21, n. 22, n. 26, n. 33 (Blackmun, J.). For an audio recording of the oral arguments in *Roe*, see http://www.oyez.org/cases/1970-1979/1971/ 1971_70_18. See also Joseph Dellapenna, *Dispelling the Myths of Abortion History* (Durham, NC: Carolina Academic Press, 2006), 14–15.

the founding era "a woman enjoyed a substantially broader right to terminate a pregnancy than she does in most States today."[17] The Court appealed to Means' historical research to support this claim. As Weddington later recalled of her reaction when the opinion was released, "I had not been reading the extensive footnotes at the bottom of each page closely, but sure enough, when I did I found several referring to Cyril Means's writings; I knew he would be pleased."[18] However, the history of the legislation at issue in *Steinberg v. Brown* (the Ohio case this chapter opened with) demonstrates the absurdity of Means' novel claim that concern for the life of the fetus is only a product of the mid-twentieth century. The record clearly demonstrates that the legislators who passed the statute in question were motivated, at least in part, by a desire to protect what they deemed to be unborn children. A report issued by the Ohio Senate Committee on Criminal Abortion and reprinted in the appendix to the state legislative journal described abortion as "child-murder" and noted that the best available scientific evidence suggested that a "foetus in utero is alive from the very moment of conception." To "extinguish the first spark of life," the committee further maintained, quoting the English physician Thomas Percival's 1803 *Medical Ethics*, "is a crime of the same nature, both against our Maker and society, as to destroy an infant, a child, or a man." The reason for the statute, which made no "unnatural and unscientific distinction" between pre-quickening and post-quickening abortion, was simple: "The willful killing of a human being, at any stage of its existence, is murder."[19]

---

[17] *Roe v. Wade*, 140–141 (Blackmun, J.).
[18] Sarah Weddington, *A Question of Choice* (New York: Penguin Books, 1993), 156–7. Weddington was also pleased with Blackmun's historical narrative. "There was, after all, I thought, a reason for including so much historical material in our brief and Supplementary Appendix, and for the extensive amicus effort" (156).
[19] *The Journal of the Senate of the State of Ohio, Fifty-Seventh General Assembly* (Columbus, OH: L. D. Myers & Bro., 1867), Appendix, 233–4.

The men who voted to approve this bill *and* ratify the Fourteenth Amendment in the same legislative session apparently saw no contradiction between the two. Nor did Federal District Judge Don Young see a contradiction between the Fourteenth Amendment and Ohio's restrictive abortion measures when he was tasked with writing the opinion in *Steinberg*. "Once human life has commenced," the Johnson appointee and self-described liberal Democrat declared, "the constitutional protections found in the Fifth and Fourteenth Amendments impose upon the state the duty of safeguarding it."[20] It was one thing to promulgate a right to marital privacy that encompassed a general right to use contraception, as the Court had done a few years earlier in *Griswold* v. *Connecticut* (1965). It was quite another to extend the principle to cover abortion. Contraception, as Young noted, is "concerned with preventing the creation of a new and independent life." But once the "preliminaries have ended, and a new life has begun," Young argued, a human being exists who may be deliberately and lawfully killed only in a situation that would otherwise justify homicide.[21] Given the substance of Judge Young's opinion and the legislative history of the Ohio abortion statute, it was needless, then, that the majority in *Roe* claimed "no case could be cited that holds that a fetus is a person within the meaning of the Fourteenth Amendment" – before citing *Steinberg* v. *Brown* to support the claim that "the word 'person,' as used in the Fourteenth Amendment, does not include the unborn.'"[22]

---

[20] *Steinberg* v. *Brown* 321 F. Supp. 741, 747 (Young, J.) (1970). See Julie A. Brenizer Klosterman, "A Tribute to Judge Don J. Young," *University of Toledo Law Review* 28 (1997), 357.

[21] Ibid., 746–47. Consistent with the Ohio statute's allowance for abortion when the life of the mother was in jeopardy, Young noted that the American legal tradition had long held that the deliberate taking of life is justified "when doing so is necessary to preserve or protect another or others."

[22] *Roe* v. *Wade*, 157–58 (Blackmun, J.).

In his seminal history of nineteenth-century abortion law, published five years after *Roe*, James Mohr initially cast doubt on some aspects of Means' history, noting that

> Means, who was openly trying in 1968 to build a case upon which New York state courts might invalidate anti-abortion legislation on the grounds that twentieth-century medicine had rendered an abortion every bit as safe or safer than a full-term delivery, was less than convincing on several points.[23]

As Mohr pointed out, the physicians who lobbied the state legislatures to pass restrictive abortion statutes in the mid-nineteenth century "felt very strongly indeed on the issue of protecting human life" and they "defended the value of human life as an absolute."[24] As a serious historian, Mohr would not obfuscate the centrality of human life to the nineteenth-century anti-abortion movement, but his ambiguous treatment of the common law in key parts of his book did further the notion that abortion was a protected liberty in the early Republic. In the year 1800, Mohr wrote, "no jurisdiction in the United States had enacted any statutes whatsoever on the subject of abortion; most forms of abortion were not illegal and those American women who wished to practice abortion did so."[25] In a reflection on the Supreme Court's decision in *Roe*, Mohr similarly concluded that the "anti-abortion laws of the late nineteenth century were the real aberrations in the history" of American abortion policy.[26]

As John Noonan noted the following year, one "peculiarity of Mohr's *Abortion in America* is to speak at times as though 'laws' in the United States did not include the common law."[27] Though in other places Mohr did recognize that abortion after quickening was always a common-law offense, his seemingly contradictory thesis that in the nineteenth century the United States had

---

[23] James Mohr, *Abortion in America*, 29.
[24] Ibid., 36.
[25] Ibid., vii.
[26] Ibid., 258.
[27] Noonan, *A Private Choice*, 193 n. 4.

transitioned "from a nation without abortion laws of any sort to a nation where abortion was legally and officially proscribed" did much to cement the myth that abortion was a traditional American liberty and that anti-abortion sentiment was merely one idiosyncrasy of the mid-nineteenth century.[28] The research of John Keown and others has demonstrated, however, that "the weight of available authority supports the view that the common law prohibited abortion, at the latest, after the fetus had become 'quick' or 'animated.'"[29]

The quickening distinction, which was abandoned in most American jurisdictions by the end of the nineteenth century, in turn "betrayed both pragmatic and metaphysical influences."[30] According to general rules of evidence, an abortion conviction required proof that the fetus was alive when the abortive act took place *and* that the abortive act was the cause of death.[31] In the absence of modern technology, quickening (or the felt movement of the fetus by his or her mother) was often the best available evidence of new life (and thus the starting point for any criminal abortion prosecution). Relatedly, a residual theory held in common by Aristotle and the Medieval Church, but disproved by nineteenth-century science, was that a distinct human being came into existence after fetal animation or movement.[32] The quickening requirement, coupled

---

[28] Mohr, *Abortion in America*, 226.

[29] John Keown, *Abortion, Doctors, and the Law: Some Aspects of the Legal Regulation of Abortion in England, 1803–1982* (New York: Cambridge University Press, 1988), 3. As Joseph Dellapenna writes, "The common law, in its early centuries, treated abortion as a crime in principle because it involved the killing of an unborn child – a tradition that continued with elaboration, but without interruption, until *Roe* changed it." Dellapenna, *Dispelling the Myths of Abortion History*, 135.

[30] John Keown, *Abortion, Doctors, and the Law*, 3.

[31] See, for example, the discussion of the elements of proof in abortion cases in Francis Wharton and Moreton Stillé, *Treatise on Medical Jurisprudence* (Philadelphia: Kay & Brother, 1855), §§346–355, 273–277.

[32] John Keown, *Abortion, Doctors, and the Law*, 3.

with the theory of animation, provided the foundation for Blackstone's oft-quoted line that life – a "right inherent by nature in every individual" – "begins in contemplation of law as soon as an infant is able to stir in his mother's womb."[33]

The anti-abortion legislation in the mid-nineteenth century, then, was not so much an aberration as a development. The principles underlying the traditional rules for abortion prosecutions at common law were twofold: (a) after a distinct human being came into existence his or her willful destruction was a serious crime, (b) provided that proof of the existence of new life and its willful destruction could be obtained. It is true that before legal rules governing abortions were written down in statutes, American judges often interpreted the common-law emphasis on quickening to preclude prosecutions for attempts at early abortion, agreeing with the Massachusetts Supreme Court that "at common law, no indictment will lie, for attempts to procure abortion until [a woman] is quick with child."[34] Statements such as this indicate that abortion, in many cases, was not considered an indictable offense before the detection of fetal movement, but this is quite different from the claim that abortion was something akin to a protected liberty (or "right" as Blackmun characterized it). Although "not punishable at common law," Chief Justice Lemuel Shaw wrote for the Massachusetts Court in *Commonwealth* v. *Parker* (1845), attempts at pre-quickening abortion were still held to be "offensive to good morals and injurious to society."[35]

Partly as a response to Chief Justice Shaw's decision, the Massachusetts legislature later passed a law making it a statutory crime to attempt to "procure the miscarriage of any woman" regardless of quickening.[36] Still, many states in

[33] William Blackstone, *Commentaries on the Laws of England: in Four Books* (Philadelphia: R. Welsh, 1902–1915), Vol. 1, 117–18.

[34] *Commonwealth* v. *Parker* 50 Mass. 263, 266–267 (1845) (Shaw, C.J.).

[35] Ibid., 268.

[36] *The General Statutes of the Commonwealth of Massachusetts* (Boston: Wright and Potter, n.d.), Chapter 165, Sec. 9.

the mid-nineteenth century did continue to rely on the quickening distinction for purposes of criminal prosecution. When it was suggested by counsel in an 1856 Iowa case that an unborn child should be protected under a statute that prohibited the killing of "any human being with malice aforethought," for example, Chief Justice (and future Senator) George Wright responded that an infant "*in ventre sa mere*" (i.e., in the womb of his mother) was "not a human being within the meaning" of Iowa's murder laws – at least "not such before it is quick in the womb."[37] As a matter of positive law, Justice Wright was perhaps correct that Iowa's murder statutes were not intended to encompass abortion – and, like Massachusetts a decade earlier, the Iowa legislature soon approved a separate ban on "foeticide" (without making a distinction for quickening).[38] Nevertheless, at least seventeen state codes in the nineteenth century *did* denominate "acts causing the death of an unborn child 'manslaughter,' 'murder,' or 'assault with intent to murder,'"[39] and by mid-century the quickening requirement was increasingly thought to be in tension with the best available science and with the principles underlying the traditional common-law categories.

As Francis Wharton explained in his mid-century treatise on criminal law,

> It has been said that it is not an indictable offence to administer a drug to a woman, and thereby to procure an abortion, unless the mother is *quick* with child, though such a distinction, it is submitted, is neither in accordance with the result of medical experience, nor with the principles of the common law.[40]

---

[37] *Abrams v. Foshee* 3 Iowa 274, 279–280 (1856) (Wright, C.J.).

[38] *Acts and Resolutions Passed at the Regular Session of the Seventh General Assembly of the State of Iowa* (Des Moines: J. Teesdale, 1858), Chapter 58.

[39] James S. Witherspoon, "Reexamining *Roe*: Nineteenth-Century Abortion Statutes and the Fourteenth Amendment," *St. Mary's Law Journal* 17 (1985), 44. For a list of state code citations, see 44 n. 47.

[40] Francis Wharton, *The Criminal Law of the United States* (Philadelphia: Kay & Brother, 1846), 308.

It was not in accordance with medical experience because the medieval theory of animation had long since been discredited, and it was not in accordance with the principles of the common law because the traditional categories had presupposed the moral axiom that one should not destroy innocent human life.[41] As Wharton wrote in a separate treatise on medical jurisprudence, the quickening distinction, undergirded by the theory of animation, was "explicable in the infancy of physiological science, by an inadequate knowledge of the development of the embryo," but it "should now, when ignorance is no longer excusable, disappear from our penal system."[42] From this perspective, then, there had been no alteration of principle in the nineteenth century – only an advance in knowledge.[43]

Motivated in large part by concerns that the public was ignorant of the emerging facts of embryology, a group of nineteenth-century physicians and lawyers began to argue that the old quickening requirement should be abandoned as arbitrary and ultimately misguided. The "whole question of the criminality" of abortion, Horatio Storer wrote in his 1868 *Criminal Abortion,*

> turns on this one fact, – the real nature of the foetus *in utero*. If the foetus be a lifeless excretion, however soon it might have received life, the offence is comparatively as *nothing*: if the foetus be already, and from the very outset, a human being alive, however early its stage of development, and existing independently of its mother, though drawing its sustenance from her, the offence becomes, in every stage of pregnancy, MURDER.[44]

From this basis, Storer criticized the traditional quickening distinction, insisting that by the common law and by many

[41] See, e.g., Horatio Robinson Storer and Franklin Fiske Heard, *Criminal Abortion: Its Nature, Its Evidence, and Its Law* (Boston: Little, Brown, and Company, 1868). On the first page of their influential treatise, Storer and Heard summarized the traditional maxim: "By the moral law, the wilful killing of a human being at any stage of its existence is murder" (1).

[42] Wharton and Stillé, *A Treatise on Medical Jurisprudence*, §283, 232.

[43] See Joseph Dellapenna, "The History of Abortion: Technology, Morality, and Law," *University of Pittsburgh Law Review* 40 (1978–79), 359–428.

[44] Storer and Heard, *Criminal Abortion*, 9–10.

of the state criminal codes "foteal life, per se, is almost wholly ignored, and its destruction unpunished; abortion, in every case, being considered an offence mainly against the mother, and as such, unless fatal to her, a mere misdemeanor, or wholly disregarded."[45]

Storer was particularly critical of the common categorization of abortion as a misdemeanor, rather than a felony, and the classification of pre-quickening abortion as a nonindictable offense,[46] but his broad claim that the law was unconcerned with fetal life was more a polemic designed to spur reform than a fair analysis of the tradition. The reality, as Joel Prentiss Bishop noted in a commentary on the criminal law published the same year, was that "the offence of abortion, as actually perpetrated or as attempted, is defined and forbidden by statutes in England, and in probably every one of our own States."[47] Yet even if Storer was correct in his analysis of the law, the arguments he and others put forward in their much maligned "crusade" against abortion serve only to reiterate the point that one of the central aims of the anti-abortion movement in the nineteenth century was emphatically to protect the lives of unborn children.

## REFRAMING THE ABORTION DEBATES

Many modern scholars, however, argue that the rhetoric of preserving fetal life has historically been bound up with the desire to preserve antiquated gender roles during times of social upheaval. In a summary of this literature Reva Siegel writes that "concerns about protecting the unborn are entangled with assumptions about sexuality and motherhood." In particular, Siegal asserts that the traditional "fetus-centered framework" conceals a desire "to compel women who are resisting motherhood to perform the work

---

[45]  Ibid., 1.
[46]  Ibid., 6–7.
[47]  Joel Prentiss Bishop, *Commentaries on the Criminal Law*, 4th ed. (Boston: Little, Brown, & Co., 1868), Vol. 2, Bk. 10, §§6–10.

of bearing and rearing children."[48] Relatedly, scholars have sought to minimize the significance of the physicians' "pro-life" rhetoric by highlighting other motivating factors in the physicians' nineteenth-century crusade against abortion – for example, the goal of regulating the practice of medicine, reversing the decline in Anglo-Protestant family sizes, preserving traditional sexual mores, and/or keeping women in domestic social roles.[49] As the *Historians' Brief* in *Webster* maintained,

> a variety of complex factors underlay the nineteenth-century laws restricting abortion: concern for women's health, the medical profession's desire to control the practice of medicine, openly discriminatory concepts of the appropriate role of women, opposition to non-procreative sexual activity and to the dissemination of information concerning birth control, and hostility to those who did not fit the white Anglo-Saxon Protestant model. Our brief shows that concern for the fetus has become a central argument for antiabortion laws only as these earlier justifications have become either anachronistic or constitutionally and culturally impermissible.[50]

Like the history pioneered by Cyril Means, the *Historians' Brief* asserted that "nineteenth-century laws restricting access to abortion were not based on a belief that the fetus is a human being" and that the "protection of fetal life" was "plainly not the driving concern" of the anti-abortion movement in the nineteenth century.[51] Rather, consistent with the new abortion history, it was claimed that the doctors leading the anti-abortion movement "sought to protect the privilege of elite white Anglo-Saxon Protestants, not to protect fetuses."[52]

---

[48] Reva Siegel, "Abortion," in Richard Wightman Fox and James T. Kloppenberg, eds., *Companion to American Thought* (Oxford: Blackwell Publishers, 1995), 2.

[49] See, for example, Sara Dubow's award-winning *Ourselves Unborn: A History of the Fetus in Modern America* (New York: Oxford University Press, 2011). Both today and in the nineteenth century, Dubow asserts, "the debate about abortion is less about the life and rights of the fetus than it is about women's role in society" (183).

[50] *Historians' Brief*, 8–9.

[51] Ibid., 43–44.

[52] Ibid., 43.

Mohr's *Abortion in America* was cited in support of these claims, and Mohr himself was among the brief's signers. As Gerard Bradley noted, however, the claim that nineteenth-century physicians were unconcerned with protecting pre-natal human life was explicitly contradicted by Mohr's published work. "Whatever the reasons," Mohr had previously written, "regular physicians felt very strongly indeed on the issue of protecting human life. And once they had decided that human life was present to some extent in a newly fertilized ovum, however limited that extent might be, they became fierce opponents of any attack upon it."[53] And yet "when reached by telephone," Bradley recounted,

> Mohr conceded that some of what the brief said and implied about the common law and the purpose of the nineteenth-century statutes was inconsistent with what he had maintained in his book. He added that where inconsistencies exist he stood by the book rather than the brief, and he confessed that he was uncomfortable with the way his work was cited for some of the brief's claims. But he went on to express the view that the brief was a "political document," the work of a "citizen" not a "scholar."[54]

The authors of the *Historians' Brief*, in other words, misused primary sources and propagated falsehoods to craft a "political" statement designed to influence a Supreme Court case. To his credit, Mohr withheld his signature from an almost identical brief submitted a few years later in *Planned Parenthood* v. *Casey*,[55] but the fact remains that some of the original signers, including Mohr, knew the historical claims were false and signed the brief anyway.

The brief's organizer, Sylvia Law, later conceded that there was "a tension between truth-telling and advocacy."[56] What she was willing to identify as the historians' "most

---

[53] Mohr, *Abortion in America*, 36.

[54] Gerard Bradley, "Academic Integrity Betrayed," *First Things* (August/September 1990).

[55] "Brief for 250 American Historians as Amici Curiae in Support of Planned Parenthood of Southeastern Pennsylvania," *Planned Parenthood* v. *Casey* 505 U.S. 833 (1992) (1992 U.S. S. Ct. Briefs LEXIS 291).

[56] Sylvia Law, "Conversations Between Historians and the Constitution," *The Public Historian* 12, no. 3 (1990), 14.

serious deficiencies as truth-tellers," however, only high-lighted her resolve to stand by the historically dubious claim that concern for fetal life was only of recent origin. While lamenting the fact that the historians had ignored the "complicated" views of nineteenth-century feminists (most, if not all, of whom expressed moral opposition to abortion[57]) and that the brief did not tell the stories of "people of color, the poor, and other marginalized groups," Law did resolutely stand by the veracity of one claim. "Plainly," she said, "no one in the eighteenth century, including the Founders, thought of the fetus as a human being."[58] In light of the myriad claims to the contrary – in medical jurisprudence textbooks, criminal law treatises, and legal commentaries – Law's assertion is simply indefensible.

Even so, the *Historians' Brief* has had a heavy influence on legal scholarship. As just one example, the second most-cited legal scholar of the twentieth century,[59] Ronald Dworkin, relied uncritically on the brief for the historical portion of his influential treatise on abortion and euthanasia. "It is true," Dworkin asserted erroneously,

> that in the nineteenth century liberal laws were replaced by laws that prohibited or strictly regulated abortion. The best historical evidence shows that these new laws were not adopted out of concern for fetuses, however, but in large part to protect the health of the mother and the privileges of the medical profession.[60]

---

[57] See Dellapenna, *Dispelling the Myths of Abortion History*, 373–387.

[58] Law, "A Conversation Between Historians and the Constitution," 15–16.

[59] Fred R. Shapiro, "The Most-Cited Legal Scholars," *Journal of Legal Studies* 29, no. 1 (2000), 424.

[60] Ronald Dworkin, *Life's Dominion* (New York: Knopf, 1993). The only reference for this claim is the *Historians' Brief*. In a footnote, Dworkin also thought it was "worth noticing that James Mohr, the historian cited in the government's brief in that case to support the claim that anti-abortion laws are traditional in America, is one of the signatories of the historians' brief" (249 n. 8). However, Mohr admitted that his research contradicted the brief, and he declined to sign a similar brief in *Casey*, which was decided a year before Dworkin published *Life's Dominion*. Interestingly, Sylvia Law cited Dworkin's reliance on the *Historians' Brief* as evidence of its successful mobilization of "elite public opinion." See Law, "A Conversation Between Historians and the Constitution," 16.

On the matter of fetal personhood, Dworkin similarly maintained (following Blackmun, who was following Means) that "American law had never in the past treated fetuses as constitutional persons."[61] Without an original analysis or even a secondary source citation, Dworkin then insisted that the "structure and detail of the anti-abortion laws show, moreover, that even the strictest states rejected the idea that a fetus is a constitutional person ... it was simply assumed that even in principle abortion is not so serious a matter as murder."[62] The historical record was so clear on this point, Dworkin asserted, that anyone who disagreed with the Supreme Court on the question of fetal personhood was simply relying on a "particularly odd and unpopular ... moral conviction" rather than good-faith historical or legal analysis.[63]

The twin notions that the common law secured a right to abortion and that the protection of unborn life was (at best) a peripheral concern in the nineteenth century have remained unchallenged by all but a few scholarly abortion histories. One section title in Janet Farrell Brodie's *Contraception and Abortion in Nineteenth-Century America* offers a succinct overview of the new abortion history: "After Two Centuries of Legality, Reproductive Control Becomes a Felony."[64] On the one hand, Brodie claims, the right to abortion promulgated in *Roe* represented a return to a traditional liberty women enjoyed under the common law. On the other hand, the anti-abortion legislation of the mid-nineteenth century was part of a broader effort orchestrated by regular physicians to

---

[61] Ibid., 110

[62] Ibid., 112.

[63] Ibid., 112.

[64] Janet Farrell Brodie, *Contraception and Abortion in Nineteenth-Century America* (Ithaca, NY: Cornell University Press, 1994), 253. For a recent presentation of this basic narrative, see N. E. H. Hull and Peter Charles Hoffer, *Roe v. Wade: The Abortion Rights Controversy in American History*, 2nd ed., revised and expanded (Lawrence: University Press of Kansas, 2010), 11–48.

gain greater control over key aspects of American life. The physicians wanted broader public respect for medicine, tighter control over who was to be allowed into the profession and what therapies they could practice. They wanted to drive out irregulars and sectarians, "quacks" and abortionists. They sought also an expanded role for physicians as moral arbiters, a role some of the regular medical professionals had aspired to since the days of Benjamin Rush, who, interested in promoting virtue in the newly created republic, envisioned physicians in the role priests held in the Old World.[65]

Of course, the physicians of the nineteenth century did push for greater regulation in the practice of medicine (thus minimizing competition from "quacks," "midwives," and other "irregulars"), but the degree to which the new histories minimize or dismiss the physicians' clear concern for unborn human life is staggering. In the "first campaigns against abortion, in the mid-nineteenth century," Linda Gordon writes, "the status of the fetus was a minor theme, and opponents of abortion did not attribute legal rights or personhood to the fetus."[66] Perhaps unsurprisingly, Gordon's sole source for this claim was the *Historians' Brief* from *Webster*.[67]

Many of the scholars adhering to the new abortion history also misrepresent the status of abortion at common law. After the successful campaign to pass restrictive abortion statutes, Leslie Reagan misleadingly claims, "women lost what had been a common-law right."[68] Similarly, Carroll Smith-Rosenberg insists that the mid-century antiabortion movement "made abortion illegal for the first time in the United States."[69] These claims, in turn, nearly all stem from Mohr's ambiguous assertion that America at its

[65] Ibid., 269–70.
[66] Linda Gordon, *The Moral Property of Women: A History of Birth Control Politics in America* (Champaign: University of Illinois Press, 2002), 305.
[67] Ibid., 418 n. 30.
[68] Leslie J. Reagan, *When Abortion was a Crime: Women, Medicine, and Law in the United States, 1867–1973* (Berkeley: University of California Press, 1997), 14.
[69] Carroll Smith-Rosenberg, *Disorderly Conduct: Visions of Gender in Victorian England* (New York: Oxford University Press, 1996), 218.

founding was a "nation without abortion laws of any sort"[70] and in the equally ambiguous assertion made in the *Historians' Brief* (citing only Blackmun and Mohr) that "abortion was not illegal at common law."[71] Less ambiguously, the Supreme Court had expressed doubt in *Roe* that "abortion was ever firmly established as a common law crime even with respect to the destruction of a quick fetus."[72]

The new histories are spun off from deliberately fabricated narratives, and rarely does anyone return to the primary sources. One aberration from this general pattern is the appeal to *State* v. *Cooper*, a case decided by the New Jersey Supreme Court in 1846.[73] The *Historians' Brief*, for example, cites this case as the sole evidence for its assertion that "nineteenth-century laws restricting access to abortion were not based on a belief that the fetus is a human being."[74] In the case, Eliakim Cooper had been indicted in Morris County for allegedly administering abortifacients to a woman and physically assaulting her with the intent to procure a miscarriage. The woman, however, claimed that she had consented to the attempted abortion, and at the time of the attempt she had not yet detected fetal movement. The "only point reserved, and submitted for the opinion of this court," the Chief Justice therefore asserted, "is whether *an attempt* to procure an abortion, the mother not being quick with child, is an indictable offense at the common law."[75] Though it had been alleged that Mr. Cooper had committed "an offence against the person of the child," the relevant question was "whether that be at all an offence or not, and whether the child be *in esse*, so that any crime can be committed against its person."[76]

---

[70] Mohr, *Abortion in America*, 226.
[71] *Historians' Brief*, 13 n. 6.
[72] *Roe* v. *Wade*, 136 (Blackmun, J.).
[73] *State* v. *Cooper* 22 N.J.L. 52 (1948). Note: The Supreme Court of New Jersey, which decided this case, was not the court of last resort.
[74] *Historians' Brief*, 44 n. 92.
[75] *State* v. *Cooper* (1849), 22 N.J.L. 52, 54 (italics in original).
[76] Ibid., 54.

The Court gave an overview of the familiar common-law sources, noting that Coke and Hale did not classify pre-quickening abortion as murder, Blackstone emphasized quickening as the point at which "life begins in contemplation of law," and that no common-law authority treated the "mere procuring of an abortion by the destruction of a *foetus* unquickened, as a crime against the person or against God and religion."[77] While it was true that for "certain civil purposes, the law regards an infant as *in being* from the time of conception," still, the Court maintained, "it seems no where to regard it as *in life*, or to have respect to its preservation as a living being."[78] Only when the "child had quickened in the womb" had that "period arrived when the life of the infant, in contemplation of law, had commenced."[79]

At first glance, the rhetoric of the New Jersey Court in *State* v. *Cooper* is perhaps the most favorable evidence that can be cited in support of the claim that nineteenth-century abortion statutes did not consider unborn children to be human beings. Yet several aspects of the case actually lead to the opposite conclusion. First, the Court was clear that prior to quickening only the *attempt* to procure abortion could be proved, as quickening was itself the "first physical proof of life."[80] Second, implicit in the Court's argument was the premise that the common law *did* consider an unborn child to be a "person *in being*" after quickening. Finally, the Court employed the Latin phrase *in esse* (i.e., in being) as a technical legal term, indicating that a child did not have an independent legal existence in criminal law (although he or she did in civil law) before evidence of fetal movement could be established. Yet the Court also admitted that the phrase "in being" was not used "with

[77] Ibid., 55.
[78] Ibid., 56.
[79] Ibid., 56.
[80] Ibid., 54.

physiological accuracy," and in *obiter dicta* the Chief Justice asserted:

> If the good of society requires that the evil [of attempted pre-quickening abortion] should be suppressed by penal inflictions, it is far better that it should be done by legislative enactments than that courts should, by judicial construction, extend the penal code or multiply the objects of criminal punishment. We deem it unwise upon this subject to occupy debatable ground.[81]

During the state legislative session later that year, New Jersey followed the suggestion of the Court by enacting an anti-abortion statute, which abandoned the quickening distinction and made it a statutory crime to "maliciously or unlawfully" *attempt* "to procure the miscarriage of a woman then pregnant with child."[82]

If anything, this case and the state statute written in response only underscore the fact that mid-century anti-abortion statutes were written (at least in part) to protect fetal life, often without regard to quickening, and often as a response to the perceived inadequacy of the traditional quickening distinction in light of new scientific evidence. In 1868, when the Fourteenth Amendment was ratified, thirty states and six territories had anti-abortion statutes on the books; twenty-seven of those states prohibited abortion attempts before quickening, eight states classified abortion as manslaughter, and the New Mexico territory deemed successful abortion to be murder.[83] Most abortion statutes were included in the section of the state codes that defined "offenses against the person," and the terms "foetus" and "child" were used interchangeably. In light of the documentary record, the most that can be said for the claim that the protection of fetal life was not a driving concern in the nineteenth century is "that it is absolutely wrong."[84]

---

[81] Ibid., 58.

[82] Lucius Elmer, *A Digest of the Laws of New Jersey*, 2nd ed. (Philadelphia: J. B. Lippencott & Co., 1855), 177–78.

[83] See Witherspoon, *Reexamining Roe*, 33 n. 15, 34 n. 18, 42 n. 34–5.

[84] Robert M. Byrn, "An American Tragedy: The Supreme Court on Abortion," *Fordham Law Review* 41 (1973): 807–862, 828.

As Cyril Means was willing to admit in 1971, "no modern American scholar" had "shown any awareness" of the thesis that abortion was a protected liberty at common law, and the same could have been said for his claim that the sole legislative purpose of anti-abortion statutes was the protection of women.[85] The reason the Supreme Court relied so uncritically on the idiosyncratic abortion history of the former lead counsel to a national organization seeking to repeal the nation's abortion laws is bound up with the obvious underlying incentives to misrepresent the historical record in the service of policy objectives. As the *Historians' Brief* in *Webster* asserted: "No Justice of this Court has seriously disputed that the wise and intended meaning of our Constitution is determined by interpreting its words in light of our nation's history and traditions."[86] In this spirit, the historians used their professional credentials to reinforce the notion that the Court's opinion in *Roe v. Wade* was based on "a rich and sound description of the history of abortion."[87] For obvious reasons, the alternative – that *Roe* was a radical break from America's history and traditions – could not be admitted.

Ironically, the historians' invocation of the legacy of *Dred Scott* in an almost identical brief submitted for *Planned Parenthood v. Casey* (1992) adds yet another thread to the tapestry of *Dred Scott/Roe* comparisons. "Because an understanding of our nation's history rightly influences this Court's fundamental constitutional understandings," the brief declares,

> it is essential to capture that history deeply and accurately. It is no accident that *Scott v. Sandford*, 19 How. 1, 19–20 (1857), and *Plessy v. Ferguson*, 163 U.S. 537, 544, 550–51 (1896) – two of this Court's most discredited decisions – rested largely on disputed and insupportable readings of history.[88]

---

[85] Means, "The Phoenix of Abortional Freedom," 352.
[86] *Historians' Brief*, 9.
[87] Ibid., 12.
[88] "Brief of 250 American Historians," *Planned Parenthood v. Casey*, 12.

*Roe* v. *Wade*, in other words, was unlike *Dred Scott* (and *Plessy*) insofar as it rested on a solid historical foundation. The implication, of course, was that *Roe*'s history was indisputable. That suggestion sheds light on why the stakes in the debates over abortion history seem so large and why participants in the abortion reform movement have been careful to circle the wagons around a historical narrative that connects *Roe* to the common law and the American founding. "The history of Anglo-American abortion laws," Joseph Dellapenna notes, "is central to the abortion controversy, serving to connect today's stories to the story of the Constitution and establishing a contemporary social context for appraising the ongoing value debates embodied in the story of abortion."[89]

## THE POLITICS OF ABORTION HISTORY

As the Supreme Court recognized in *Casey*, "for two decades of economic and social developments, people have organized intimate relationships and made choices that define their views of themselves and their places, in reliance on the availability of abortion in the event that contraception should fail."[90] Replacing two decades with four, the same observation could be made today. The Supreme Court's landmark decision in *Roe* – though perennially divisive and controversial – is a central factor in the profound social and economic transformations that have occurred in America since the 1970s. Though the constitutional narrative that undergirded the Supreme Court's abortion jurisprudence in *Roe* was largely false, the construction of that narrative was a critical aspect of the initial creation, and subsequent maintenance, of constitutional abortion rights in the late twentieth century.

---

[89] Dellapenna, *Dispelling the Myths of Abortion History*, 12.
[90] *Planned Parenthood* v. *Casey* 505 U.S. 833, 856 (1992) (O'Connor, Kennedy, and Souter, JJ.).

In a subsequent reflection on the *Historians' Brief*, James Mohr was willing to concede that he did not "ultimately consider the brief to be history, as I understand the craft."[91] History was messier, "full of complexity, paradox, nuance, and ambiguity."[92] In contrast, a legal brief was a "political document"[93] written by lawyers with the need to "minimize nuance, ambiguity, or the serious consideration of countervailing evidence, precisely because they ultimately care less for what the past might teach us in the abstract than they do for what the past might do to help us achieve a desired result in the present, since that was the lawyer's purpose in turning to the past in the first place."[94] Although the brief's stated aim was to "provide a rich and accurate description of our national history and traditions," Mohr was remarkably open about the fact that the true objective was to politically shore up and safeguard the constitutional right pronounced by the Supreme Court in *Roe*. Mohr defended this political exercise because, in his view, the opponents of abortion also had been weaving simplistic historical narratives to suit their political agendas, and the *Historians' Brief* comported "more fully" with his "understanding of the past than the historical arguments mounted on the other side."[95]

Mohr therefore threw the weight of his credentials behind the brief even as aspects of his own research cut against the central claim that concern for the life of the fetus was a new phenomenon in American politics.[96] Another signer, as well, publicly took issue with the related claim that "abortion was not uncommon in colonial America."[97] In Estelle Freedman's published work on the history of American sexuality, she noted that the evidence of abortion in the

[91] James Mohr, "Historically Based Legal Briefs: Observations of a Participant in the *Webster* Process," *The Public Historian* 12, no. 3 (1990), 25.
[92] Ibid., 24.
[93] Ibid., 25.
[94] Ibid., 20.
[95] Ibid., 25.
[96] See Mohr, *Abortion in America*, 35–36.
[97] *Historians' Brief*, 15.

late eighteenth century was scant. The general mores of
society, she insisted, sought to "contain sexuality within a
reproductive framework, for both economic and religious
reasons" and, as a result, "neither contraception nor abortion was very important."[98] Infanticide, she suggested, was
the more common means of controlling reproduction in
colonial America, and this was always condemned.[99] The
two central claims of the new abortion history – that the
purpose of anti-abortion laws was not to protect the unborn
and that abortion was common and legal throughout most
of American history – were thus directly contradicted by the
research of two of the brief's most prominent signers.

As David Tundermann acknowledged in a memo circu-
lated among Norma McCorvey's legal team, the purpose of
Means' history (and the subsequent historiography built
upon it) was to preserve "the guise of impartial scholarship
while advancing the proper ideological goals."[100] The fact
that Tundermann identified some of the serious flaws
in Means' research *before* Sarah Weddington decided to
emphasize its importance at the bar of the Supreme Court
is noteworthy, but not surprising, given the obvious utility
of this simplistic historical narrative. Although the history
undergirding the landmark opinion in *Roe* has quietly
faded to the background of the Court's most recent abortion
cases,[101] the constitutional narrative constructed by Means
served as both the scaffolding and ideological frame for the

---

[98] Estelle B. Freedman, "Historical Interpretation and Legal Advocacy:
     Rethinking the *Webster* Amicus Brief," *The Public Historian* 12, no. 3
     (1990), 29. See John D'Emilio and Estelle B. Freedman, *Intimate Matters: A
     History of Sexuality in America* (New York: Harper and Row, 1988).
[99] Ibid., 29.
[100] Memo from David Tundermann to Roy Lucas, "Legislative Purpose et al.," 5
     August 1971, cited in David Garrow, *Liberty and Sexuality: The Right to
     Privacy and the Making of* Roe v. Wade (Berkeley: University of California
     Press [1994] 1998), 891–892, n. 41.
[101] For example, compare Blackmun's *Roe* opinion with his partial concurrence/
     partial dissent in *Planned Parenthood* v. *Casey*. Notice also the dearth of
     historical arguments in *Stenberg* v. *Carhart* 530 U.S. 914 (2000) and
     *Gonzales* v. *Carhart* 550 U.S. 124 (2007).

Court's early abortion jurisprudence. Understandably, proponents of abortion rights have shifted focus in an attempt to provide alternative constitutional foundations, but the new abortion narrative remains an important component of the political construction and maintenance of constitutional abortion rights.

Equally important to the creation of a constitutional right to abortion in the twentieth century was the ideological shift in elite segments of society with respect to the value placed on individual human lives as such. In his seminal history of nineteenth-century abortion policy, Mohr noted that the nation's physicians "defended the value of human life per se as an absolute." Tabling the question of *why* the physicians defended human life in such a way, Mohr suggested that future scholars "interested in the medical mentality of the nineteenth century will have to explain the reasons for this ideological position." In so framing the issue, Mohr implied that the physicians' opposition to abortion was aberrational from the mainstream of the American moral and political tradition. The impetus for the physicians' crusade against abortion was, however, based on empirical, rather than ideological, developments. In other words, the physicians' "defense of human life per se as an absolute" was not innovative. The rhetorical strategy of the physicians was not to convince their readers that deliberate killing was wrong but rather that modern science had demonstrated that human life began much sooner than many believed. The explicit defense of abortion as justifiable homicide has emerged only recently, but this ideological change has been obscured by a deliberately distorted historical narrative.

Relatedly, the common characterization of the abortion debates as inherently religious or metaphysical has subtly shifted how we frame and understand the controversy. If abortion is at root a religious issue, it is often contended, then it is illegitimate in our politically liberal society to impose subjective religious beliefs about abortion on others.

As Stephen Douglas said of slavery, many today say of abortion: Our fellow citizens "bear consciences as well as we" and, like us, are "accountable to God" for their own moral decisions.[102] The coherence of this position, however, depends on an answer to the very moral question it refuses to engage. Public policy can no more remain neutral with respect to the morality of abortion than it can with respect to the morality of slavery. As Lincoln insisted in response to Douglas, the contention that "whoever wants slaves" has "a right to have them" is "perfectly logical if there is nothing wrong in the institution; but if you admit that it is wrong, he cannot logically say anybody has a right to do wrong."[103] Like slavery, the right to abortion is perfectly logical if the object of the act is not a human being or if human beings at some early stage of development are not moral persons. Yet the feigned neutrality of liberal public reason prevents engagement with such questions and screens from view the essential continuity of the pro-life argument, stretching from the nineteenth century to today.

[102] Roy P. Basler, ed., *Collected Works of Abraham Lincoln*, 8 vols. (New Brunswick, NJ: Rutgers University Press, 1953), Vol. 3, 274.
[103] Ibid., 257.

# 6

## Private Morality, Public Reasons

"The anti-choice people all ask me," Norma McCorvey told a *New York Times* reporter in the mid-1990s, "When do I think life begins?" "I don't know," she insisted, "I'm not a rocket scientist."[1] The *Times* piece profiled McCorvey's 1994 memoir *I Am Roe*, and the article hit newsstands in July of the same year. A little more than twelve months later McCorvey committed her life to "serving the Lord and helping women save babies."[2] The radical and sudden reorientation of her politics occurred after accepting an unlikely invitation to attend church with an evangelical member of the pro-life group Operation Rescue. A year after the *Times* showed McCorvey lamenting that she "never had the privilege to go into an abortion clinic, lay down and have an abortion," Operation Rescue's director, Phillip Bentham, baptized her on national television. "She's like Harriet Beecher Stowe, who wrote that book on slavery," Bentham later told CNN, referring to the anti-slavery novel *Uncle Tom's Cabin*.[3] The analogy was suggestive, for the evangelical Stowe's provocative and inflammatory novel

---

[1] Alex Witchel, "At Home with Norma McCorvey; Of *Roe*, Dreams, and Choices," *The New York Times* (July 28, 1994).

[2] Douglas S. Wood, "Who is 'Jane Roe'?" CNN (online), http://www.cnn.com/2003/LAW/01/21/mccorvey.interview.

[3] Ibid.

was the second bestselling book of the nineteenth century, behind only the Bible, and it "helped lay the groundwork for the Civil War."[4]

The entire episode of McCorvey's conversion also suggested something else – that her new position on abortion was bound up with her new religion. Although antiabortion arguments can be (and often are) made without reference to any religious text or tradition, religious communities have provided much of the muscle for the antiabortion movement in the United States, and individual beliefs about public policy matters are part of a thicket of personal commitments that are not always easy to untangle. This perhaps contributes to the tendency to characterize abortion as inherently a religious issue. And if abortion truly can be boiled down to religion, as Ronald Dworkin and others have insisted, then it would seem that the state has "no business prescribing what people should think about the ultimate point and value of human life, about why life has intrinsic importance, and about how that value is respected or valued in different circumstances."[5] Although one might respect McCorvey's deep convictions and change of heart as a personal religious matter, the argument goes, it would be inappropriate, in a secular and liberal society, for her to impose those beliefs on others. This popular line of argument has an academic pedigree rooted in the theory of public reason developed by the twentieth century's foremost political philosopher, John Rawls.

Rawls' subtly influential and wide-ranging political philosophy takes its bearings from the deep and intractable moral disagreements that characterize modern liberal democracies. The normal result of democracy and its "culture of free institutions," Rawls suggested, is the existence of a "plurality of conflicting reasonable comprehensive doctrines,

---

[4] Will Kaufman, *The Civil War in American Culture* (Edinburgh: Edinburgh University Press, 2006), 18.

[5] Ronald Dworkin, *Life's Dominion: An Argument About Abortion, Euthanasia, and Individual Freedom* (New York: Alfred A. Knopf, 1993), 164–5.

religious, philosophical, and moral."[6] This plurality of reasonable but conflicting comprehensive doctrines creates a practical political problem for modern democracies: Without resorting to violence, how do we collectively decide on the proper use of political power when the community itself is divided about fundamental principles of justice and the good life? Beginning with what he called the "fact of reasonable pluralism," Rawls set out to construct a workable theory of public deliberation that would illustrate the "kinds of reasons we may reasonably give one another when fundamental political questions are at stake."[7]

The theoretical apparatus that governs the kinds of reasons we, as democratic citizens, should offer those with whom we have deep disagreements about matters of basic justice is what Rawls referred to as "public reason." Rather than bringing to bear on fundamental political questions the whole truth as we see it, we ought to offer reasons that are found in an overlapping consensus shared by all reasonable citizens. In so doing, Rawls taught, we appeal to a public conception of justice shared in common with and freely embraced by others. Put another way: Reasonable citizens should set aside (at least in public debate) those aspects of their deeper worldview that are not part of the store of public reasons. Ideally, a widespread commitment to public reason would then dissolve the problem of political conflict among adherents of reasonable, but mutually exclusive, doctrines.

Yet, as more than a few of Rawls's critics have suggested, it is not obvious why, from the perspective of the deeply religious or philosophically committed person, we ought to be willing to set aside our fundamental religious or philosophical commitments when deliberating about questions of basic justice. Addressing this initial objection, Rawls asserted,

---

[6] John Rawls, *The Law of Peoples* (Cambridge, MA: Harvard University Press, 1993), 131.
[7] Ibid., 132.

Political liberalism replies: our exercise of political power is proper and hence justifiable only when it is exercised in accordance with a constitution the essentials of which all citizens may reasonably be expected to endorse in the light of principles and ideals acceptable to them as reasonable and rational. This is the liberal principle of legitimacy. And since the exercise of political power itself must be legitimate, the ideal of citizenship imposes a moral, not a legal, duty – the duty of civility – to be able to explain to one another on those fundamental questions how the principles and policies they advocate and vote for can be supported by the political values of public reason.[8]

In other words, the reason we should not invoke our private conceptions of justice – rooted in a contested comprehensive doctrine or worldview – is because of what Rawls referred to as the liberal principle of legitimacy and the duty of civility. Rawls derived these, in turn, from the notion of democratic citizens as free and equal moral persons engaged in a system of social cooperation over time, a notion that was "worked up" (i.e., socially and politically constructed) from the "public political culture of a democratic society, in its basic political texts (constitutions and declarations of human rights), and in the historical tradition of the interpretation of those texts."[9] In this way, Rawls maintained, his theory of public reason was "part of the idea of democracy itself" even as it remained unmoored from any particular philosophic or religious foundation.[10] This was, for Rawls, one of public reason's great virtues: Adherents of various comprehensive doctrines could embrace it even though it did not depend on any one comprehensive doctrine for its epistemological foundation.

## SLAVERY, ABORTION, AND PUBLIC DEBATE

At his most concise, Rawls proposed that "in public reason comprehensive doctrines of truth or right be replaced by an

---

[8] John Rawls, *Political Liberalism* (New York: Columbia University Press, 1993), 217.
[9] John Rawls, *Justice as Fairness: A Restatement* (Cambridge, MA: Harvard University Press, 2001), 18–24.
[10] Rawls, *Law of Peoples*, 131.

idea of the politically reasonable addressed to citizens as citizens."[11] One charge leveled at the whole idea of public reason, as it was constructed by Rawls, however, is that the wisdom of "bracketing moral and religious controversies for the sake of political agreement" must depend on whether either one of "the contending moral and religious doctrines is true."[12] In one notable example, Rawls's Harvard colleague Michael Sandel suggested that the

> difficulty of asserting the priority of "political values" without reference to the claims of morality and religion can be seen by considering two political controversies that bear on grave moral and religious questions. One is the contemporary debate about abortion rights. The other is the famous debate between Abraham Lincoln and Stephen Douglas over popular sovereignty and slavery.[13]

The politics of slavery and abortion put maximum pressure on Rawls's theory of public reason, because the political resolution of each issue depends – unavoidably – on contested notions of the good and right. Additionally, both issues provide a wealth of examples drawn from practical politics that help illuminate the application, and ultimate weakness, of the doctrine of public reason. To highlight one example, salient aspects of the abortion/slavery analogy boiled to the surface of national debate when Bob Dole called for a "declaration of tolerance" toward pro-choice Republicans at the 1996 party convention. "If, as Dole admits, abortion is a moral question on which people disagree," Sandel asked in the pages of *The New Republic*, "why not let each decide the question for herself? Why insist that the federal government should impose on some the moral convictions of others?" The answer, coming by way of analogy to slavery, was that "it is difficult to separate

[11] Ibid., 132.
[12] Michael Sandel, "Book Review: *Political Liberalism*," *Harvard Law Review* 107 (1994), 1776.
[13] Ibid., 1777. See also Stephen Macedo's response to Sandel in "In Defense of Liberal Public Reason: Are Slavery and Abortion Hard Cases?" *The American Journal of Jurisprudence* (1997), 1–29.

toleration of the practice from toleration of those who would permit it." "If abortion is murder," Sandel insisted, "those who would tolerate it are no more worthy of respect then those who would tolerate slavery."[14]

Sandel is pro-choice, and he ultimately agrees with Rawls's position that abortion, in most circumstances, ought to be a protected liberty. The disagreement between the two Harvard professors was about whether it is feasible or appropriate to entertain a private belief that a certain practice is gravely immoral – say, slavery or abortion – but nevertheless agree to bracket that belief in public debate about government policy. The analogy with the nineteenth-century debate over slavery is powerful, in part, because of its rhetorical similarities with the current debate over abortion. For both issues, there is an inherent contradiction in saying, "I believe X is wrong; but I also think people should be allowed to do X." For some issues, like smoking or gambling or working on Sunday, this position may be perfectly viable. But for slavery or abortion, because of the gravity of what is at stake, the formula inevitably rings hollow.

Consider the argument former New York City Mayor and presidential candidate Rudy Giuliani gave to an audience at Houston Baptist University in 2007. In an attempt to explain his pro-choice position to socially conservative voters, Giuliani insisted he personally believed abortion to be "morally wrong." Yet "people of good faith, people who are equally decent, equally moral, and equally religious," he noted, "come to different conclusions about" the issue. In the face of such reasonable disagreement, Giuliani said he would "respect their viewpoint" and grant them "the right to make that choice."[15] Giuliani's attempt to blend moral disapproval of abortion with support for its protection as a matter of private choice was, of course, not a novelty.

---

[14] Michael Sandel, "The Hard Questions: Tolerating the Tolerant," *The New Republic* (July 15 & 22, 1996), 25.

[15] Rudy Giuliani, "In His Own Words," *The New York Times* (May 12, 2007), http://www.nytimes.com/2007/05/12/us/politics/12rudyword.html.

Pro-choice candidates for national office routinely declare themselves to be personally opposed to abortion while defending it, as Giuliani did, as a lamentable but private "decision between a woman, her doctor, her family and her God."[16] Even so, if Mayor Giuliani was willing to insist that abortion was "morally wrong" while declaring himself to be pro-choice, the questions properly arose: What is the nature of the wrong and why should the law protect it?

On this score, Giuliani unconsciously echoed Stephen Douglas. Abortion was not a national political issue during Douglas's career, but the morally divisive issue of the extension of slavery into the federal territories was, and central to that debate was the issue of the moral status of slavery itself. Although insisting that he was not a pro-slavery man, Douglas nevertheless reasoned that the people of the slave-holding states were equally civilized, equally equipped with moral consciences, and equally accountable to God. As the Illinois Senator declared, "It is for them to decide therefore the moral and religious right of slavery for themselves within their own limits."[17] In response, Lincoln maintained that Douglas's position was logical if there was nothing wrong in slavery. But if one admitted that slavery was wrong and considered the nature of the wrong, one could not logically assert the right of one man to enslave another man as a matter of private choice. Any way one turned the Democratic policy, Lincoln asserted, there was "a careful, studied exclusion of the idea that there is anything wrong in slavery."[18] The real issue, Lincoln declared elsewhere, was whether the slave "is *not* or *is* a man," and, if he was a man, then there was no argument that would furnish a justification for his enslavement that would not, in the end, descend

---

[16] The quote comes from Giuliani's campaign website, as reported in Robin Toner, "Can the G.O.P. accept Giuliani's Abortion Stance?" *The New York Times* (May 11, 2007), http://www.nytimes.com/2007/05/11/us/politics/11record.html.

[17] Roy P. Basler, ed., *Collected Works of Abraham Lincoln*, 8 vols. (New Brunswick, NJ: Rutgers University Press, 1953), Vol. 3, 274.

[18] Ibid., Vol. 3, 257.

into a mere assertion of power or self-interest, for there could be "no moral right in connection with one man's making a slave of another."[19] Lincoln argued, in other words, that the moral status of slavery, which hinged on the human status of the enslaved, was logically prior to any question about the justice of allowing someone to own slaves or the prudence of brokering a political compromise with those with whom one harbored deep moral disagreements. Was it not a "false statesmanship," Lincoln asked in his final debate with Douglas, "that undertakes to build a system of policy upon the basis of caring nothing about *the very thing that everybody does care the most about*?"[20]

Like the debate over slavery, public deliberation about abortion depends on a judgment about the nature of the wrong in question. But the frequent insistence that moral or religious arguments in opposition to abortion are inadmissible in public deliberation has done much to obscure the actual terms of political debate in America today. In reality, pro-choice thinkers often characterize the public policy issue as indissolubly religious or metaphysical and pro-life thinkers often appeal to the empirical evidence of the hard sciences. Of course, in some sense, both sides are right. The principle that innocent human life should not be deliberately taken is a foundational moral axiom, underived and undemonstrable from the methods of modern science. Nothing we are able to observe about the physical world will establish that principle for us – it is, in this sense, metaphysical – and if the principle is denied, there can be no moral argument. The debate, if it is in good faith, is foremost about whether the object of abortion is the kind of being to which the moral axiom against deliberate killing applies. And to "say nothing about this question," William Voegeli contends rightly, "is to say nothing about the abortion issue."[21]

---

[19] Ibid., Vol. 2, 265–266 (italics in original).
[20] Ibid., Vol. 3, 311 (italics in original).
[21] William Voegeli, "A Critique of the Pro-Choice Argument," *Review of Politics* 43, no. 4 (1981), 566.

## PUBLIC REASONS AND GOD'S REASONS

When we circle back to consider this question, we do nonetheless become embroiled in a moral and theological quandary. Many (but certainly not all) people on the pro-life side today, like many of the abolitionists, base their policy position, ultimately, on what they believe to be the revealed will of God. And, as Robert George noted during a famous exchange at the 1998 American Political Science Association annual meeting,

> Anyone who believes that God has revealed that the public policy of a certain polity must be settled in a certain way has, so far as he can tell, an absolute, indefeasible reason for supporting that way of settling public policy irrespective of whether there are any grounds apart from revelation for the policy. My scruples, or Rawls's, would – and should – simply cut no ice for a person in this position.[22]

The contention that public policy debates should proceed by reference to arguments that are accessible to all reasonable people, independent of particular religious doctrines, will appear unreasonable to someone who believes that God has in fact decreed – for reasons impenetrable by the human mind – that public policy should be settled in a particular way. "It seems to me, then," George concluded, "that our differences with" people who claim esoteric knowledge about God's will for national or state policy "implicate in this way certain theological judgments."[23]

The theological judgments to which George alludes have been worked out over time, beginning with the dilemma posed by Plato in the *Euthyphro*. Either the gods love things because they are good, Socrates suggested, or things are good because the gods love them. The theoretical problem still holds in monotheistic traditions, and each horn of the

---

[22] Robert P. George, "God's Reasons: The Role of Religious Authority in Debates on Public Policy," presentation at the 1998 American Political Science Association Convention. A revised and expanded version is available at http://orthodoxytoday.org/articles/GeorgeGodsReasons.php.
[23] Ibid.

dilemma, as C. S. Lewis noted in an essay written during World War II, is equally unsatisfying:

> If the first, if good is to be defined as what God commands, then the goodness of God Himself is emptied of meaning and the commands of an omnipotent fiend would have the same claim on us as those of the "righteous Lord." If the second, then we seem to be admitting a cosmic dyarchy, or even making God himself the mere executor of a law somehow external and antecedent to His own being.[24]

Both views are practically and theoretically problematic, and, as George noted, "Many, perhaps most, serious religious believers in our society have a different understanding."[25] The third way worked out in the Western tradition is to propose a unity between God and goodness such that God has moral reasons for His actions that are part of His own nature. Human beings, made in the image of God, can thus offer one another arguments about good and choice-worthy courses of action that are rationally intelligible independent of revelation. This, broadly, is what natural law theorists have in mind when they speak of natural law as a participation in the eternal (rather than divinely revealed) law.[26]

One implication is that human beings, when they are acting rationally, make practical decisions based on some set of apprehended goods and that it *cannot* be otherwise. Consider the argument offered by Rawls that the moral duty of civility requires that we offer reasons in public debate that are found in an overlapping consensus among reasonable comprehensive doctrines. As Joseph Raz observes,

> To come to the view that one should rely on consensual principles ... is to come to a moral view and to rely on it. There is no other way. So long as we are rational in our actions, each one

[24] C. S. Lewis, "The Poison of Subjectivism," in Walter Hooper, ed., *Christian Reflections* (Grand Rapids, MI: Wm. B. Eerdmans Publishing Co., 1995), 79.

[25] George, "God's Reasons."

[26] This, of course, does not mean that reason and revelation are in tension. Indeed, traditional natural law theorists operate under the assumption that "reason and revelation are in intimate converse, each one entangled with the other." See J. Budziszewski, *The Line Through the Heart* (Wilmington, DE: ISI Books, 2009), 42.

of us can act only for reasons we believe to justify our action. Deferring to consensus is no exception.[27]

Similarly, any public policy argument about abortion will rely – explicitly or implicitly – on a normative judgment about the morality of killing at various stages of human life. Neutrality in the face of such a question is impossible. Prior to law, ethics, and theology, we simply must start with some understanding of what constitutes a human being and some consideration of what characteristics are essential to a human being's status as the bearer of rights or the object of moral duties.

Religious communities have, of course, done much to mobilize opposition to abortion, but academics often go too far in conflating the anti-abortion cause with religious dogma. Sandel, for example, insists:

> If the doctrine of the Catholic Church is true, if human life in the relevant moral sense does begin at conception, then bracketing the moral-theological question of when human life begins is far less reasonable than it would be on rival moral and religious assumptions.[28]

But in characterizing the debate in this way, Sandel runs the risk of making opposition to abortion tantamount to a private sectarian belief. In reality, most of the intelligent arguments against abortion do not depend at all on religious authority, and there is an essential continuity between the natural law arguments offered by the Catholic Magisterium today and the arguments put forward in the nineteenth century by the (largely Protestant) doctors who led the organized movement to enact strict anti-abortion laws at the state level. In both instances, the moral opprobrium attached to the act of abortion was (and is) often strengthened by religious and theological commitments, but in

[27] Joseph Raz, "Disagreement in Politics," *American Journal of Jurisprudence* 43 (1998), 27.
[28] Michael Sandel, *Liberalism and the Limits of Justice* (New York: Cambridge University Press, 1982), 198.

neither case is the question of "when human life begins" inherently religious.

## SCIENCE AND THE PRO-LIFE ARGUMENT

Frederick Dyer notes that "hundreds of physicians took up the crusade" against criminal abortion in the nineteenth century "primarily because they believed unborn children must not be sacrificed unless the life of the mother was truly at stake."[29] A large part of the physicians' rhetoric focused on empirics rather than morality, philosophy, or religion. The common-law tradition always treated abortion as a serious crime after the point of quickening, but scientific developments in the nineteenth century had shown the quickening distinction to be physiologically irrelevant. "The absurdity of the principle upon which these distinctions are founded is of easy demonstration," one medical jurisprudence textbook, in its eleventh printing by 1860, asserted.

> The foetus, previous to the time of quickening, must be either dead or living. Now, that it is not the former, is most evident from neither putrefaction nor decomposition taking place, which would be the inevitable consequences of an extinction of the vital principle. To say that the connection with the mother prevents this, is wholly untenable; facts are opposed to it. Foetuses do actually die in the uterus before quickening, and then all the signs of death are present. The embryo, therefore, before that crisis, must be in a state different from that of death, and this can be no other than life.[30]

Because the medical and legal establishment presupposed the moral axiom against killing innocent human beings, the

---

[29] Frederick N. Dyer, *The Physicians' Crusade Against Abortion* (Sagamore Beach, MA: Science History Publications, 2005), 8.

[30] Theodric Romeyn Beck and John B. Beck, *Elements of Medical Jurisprudence*, 11th ed. (Philadelphia: J. B. Lippincott & Co., 1860), 463. The text continues: "Indeed, no other doctrine appears to be consonant with reason or physiology, but that which admits the embryo to possess vitality from the very moment of conception" before citing Thomas Percival's famous line that "to extinguish the first spark of life is a crime of the same nature, both against our Maker and society, as to destroy an infant, a child, or a man" (464).

physicians involved with the anti-abortion movement in the nineteenth century thought a demonstration that life begins at conception was sufficient to establish the wrongness of abortion at any point during pregnancy. As Dr. Gunning Bedford, a professor of obstetrics at the University of New York and the nephew of one of the Constitution's original signers, asserted: "It is manifest that the moral part of the question turns upon the simple interrogatory – is the embryo in the earlier states of its existence a living being?" The answer, of course, was "yes," for "all correct physiology demonstrates that it becomes in truth, at the very moment of fecundation, imbued with vitality."[31] While Congress was drafting the Fourteenth Amendment and the Civil Rights Act of 1866, the *United States Medical and Surgical Journal* published an essay on abortion that simply declared, "The true scientific position is this: from the moment of conception, when the spermatozoa coalesces with the cell-wall of the ovule, the ovum is a distinct human being."[32]

The science has changed little in the intervening years. When *Roe v. Wade* was docketed at the Supreme Court, the state of Texas submitted a brief that contained a detailed section on embryological development. The "attack on the Texas statute," the brief maintained, "assumes the discredited scientific concept [that the conceptus is biologically indistinct from its mother until a certain point of development, e.g., quickening or viability] and argues that

[31] Gunning S. Bedford, *The Principles and Practice of Obstetrics* (New York: Samuel S. & William Wood, 1861), 678. Bedford's uncle, of the same name, was one of Delaware's delegates to the Philadelphia Convention in 1787 and a signer of the Constitution.

[32] William Henry Holcombe, "A Systematic Treatise on Abortion," *United States Medical and Surgical Journal* 1 (July 1866), 387. Holcombe also insists that the human being at this stage has "a human soul" and is "simply attached to the other for the obtainment of nutritive material, but growing, living, organizing, by forces and powers entirely its own, and derived through nature from God." While some may object that this is indeed a religious argument, it actually provides a good example of how religious arguments worked in concert with empirical observation. The question, "when does life begin?" was answered with scientific evidence, and only then was the moral/religious implication brought to bear.

abortions should be considered no differently than any medical measure taken to protect maternal health."[33] But as the Supreme Court of New York noted in a 1953 tort case involving injuries to an unborn infant, "We know something more of the actual process of conception and fetal development now than when some of the common law cases were decided; and what we know makes it possible to demonstrate clearly that separability begins at conception."[34] What could be gleaned from modern science in the mid- and late twentieth century was merely a confirmation of the empirical observations of the nineteenth-century physicians.

The Texas brief contained a detailed description of the process of fetal development accompanied by intra-uterine images of the developing young at various stages. Given the state of scientific knowledge when *Roe* was decided, there could be no real disagreement about when biological life began. During the third month of gestation – a time in which the Supreme Court insisted a state had no legitimate interest in preserving "potential" life – the child, as the brief noted, "can kick his legs, turn his feet, curl and fan his toes, make a fist, move his thumb, bend his wrist, turn his head, squint, frown, open his mouth, press his lips tightly together."[35] Moving backward chronologically to the seventh week, the "fetal heart is functioning complete and normal" and the fetus "bears the familiar external features and all the internal organs of the adult."[36] At the end of the first month, before many women even know they are pregnant, "the primary brain is present and the eyes, ears and nasal organs have started to form,"[37] and in the first weeks "the foundation of the brain, spinal cord, nerves, and sense organs is

[33] Brief for Appellee, *Roe* v. *Wade*, 31.
[34] *Kelly* v. *Gregory* 125 N.Y.S. 2d 696, 697 (1953). Cited in ibid., 31. Note: The Supreme Court of New York was not the court of last resort.
[35] Brief for Appellee, *Roe* v. *Wade*, 41.
[36] Ibid., 36.
[37] Ibid., 34.

completely formed."[38] After conception, Texas argued, there simply was no non-arbitrary point on this developmental continuum to declare that a non-human entity has suddenly become a human being. In the forty years since *Roe*, scientific advancements have only confirmed what the Texas brief referred to as the "human-ness of the fetus." As one current embryology textbook explains, "*Human development begins at fertilization* when a male gamete or sperm (spermatozoon) unites with a female gamete or oocyte (ovum) to produce a single cell – a *zygote*. This highly specialized, totipotent cell marked the beginning of each of us as a unique individual."[39] Summarizing the findings of modern embryology, Robert George and Christopher Tollefsen similarly assert, "A human embryo is not something different in kind from a human being, like a rock, or a potato, or a rhinoceros. A human embryo is a whole living member of the species Homo sapiens in the earliest stage of his or her natural development."[40] Of course the moral argument depends on the premise that human life, whenever it begins, should not be deliberately destroyed except in the direst of circumstances. And today, as in the nineteenth century, this premise is a moral axiom underived from empirical observation and often attributed to the moral law or the law of God or nature. As one of the leaders of the physicians' crusade against abortion, Horatio Storer, maintained, "By that higher than human law, which, though scoffed at by many a tongue, is yet acknowledged by every conscience,

---

[38] Ibid., 33.

[39] Keith L. Moore and T. V. N. Persaud, *The Developing Human*, 7th ed. (New York: W. B. Saunders, 2003), 34. Cited in Robert P. George and Christopher Tollefsen, *Embryo: A Defense of Human Life* (New York: Doubleday, 2008), 222 n. 9. George and Tollefsen note that this categorical finding needs to be qualified because of the phenomenon of twinning, for "identical twins do not come into existence at fertilization ... at least one embryo comes into existence at a stage later than fertilization." Still, the authors note, "this qualification has no bearing on the following point ... when someone destroys a human embryo, it is a human being that is killed" (55).

[40] George and Tollefsen, *Embryo*, 50.

'the wilful killing of a human being, at any stage of its existence, is murder.'"[41]

## THE AXIOMS OF A FREE SOCIETY

The axiom against deliberately killing innocent persons (at least in connection with the abortion debate) is rarely questioned. What is contested, however, is the notion that the unborn are fully human persons, deserving of respect in the same way as an infant or adult member of the species. The truism from Thomas Percival's 1803 *Medical Ethics* is here reversed. "To extinguish the first spark of life," Percival taught, in a formula repeated by physicians and state legislators in the nineteenth century, "is a crime of the same nature, both against our Maker and society, as to destroy an infant, a child, or a man."[42] Many – perhaps most – modern theorists, however, would agree with Sandel's contention that the "fact that every person began life as an embryo does not prove that embryos are persons."[43] Sandel, who served on the President's Counsel on Bioethics from 2002 to 2005, draws an analogy between acorns and oak trees to make his case. "[A]lthough every oak tree was once an acorn," Sandel insists,

> it does not follow that acorns are oak trees, or that I should treat the loss of an acorn eaten by a squirrel in my front yard as the same kind of loss as the death of an oak tree felled by a storm. Despite their developmental continuity, acorns and oak trees are different kinds of things. So are human embryos and human beings.[44]

Sandel also contends that the understanding of embryos as a different *kind* of thing than a human being comports more fully with how we actually treat embryos, since the logical implications of truly regarding embryos as human beings

---

[41]   Horatio Robinson Storer, *Why Not? A Book for Every Woman* (Boston: Lee & Shepard, 1866), 29.

[42]   Thomas Percival, *Medical Ethics* (Manchester, UK: S. Russell, 1803), 79.

[43]   Michael Sandel, "Embryo Ethics – The Moral Logic of Stem-Cell Research," *The New England Journal of Medicine* (July 15, 2004), 208.

[44]   Ibid., 208.

would call into question embryonic stem-cell research, the routine discarding of spare embryos left unused in fertility treatments, and the relatively casual attitude we take with regard to an early miscarriage compared to the loss of a newborn or an infant.

There is, however, something too quick about Sandel's argument from socially awkward or undesirable consequences, since the premises say more about our own attitudes and feelings than the nature of the thing in question. "It is impossible for us to suppose these creatures to be men," Montesquieu wrote satirically of African slaves in the eighteenth century, "because, allowing them to be men, a suspicion would follow that we ourselves are not Christians."[45] Sandel's argument can be reduced to a similar formula: If we supposed embryos to be full human beings, he suggests, we would then have to conclude that we are not true egalitarians, which of course is to say nothing about whether embryos are human beings. The analogy between acorns and embryos is similarly unhelpful. As Robert George and Patrick Lee pointed out in response to Sandel, "A human embryo is a human being in the embryonic stage, just as an infant or an adolescent is a human being in the infant or adolescent stage."[46] If Sandel's illustration involving our attitudes toward acorns proves anything, it proves too much. For we consider it a comparatively small loss to lose an oak sapling – which is roughly parallel to an infant in the analogy. Does this mean a sapling is different in kind than an oak or, more to the point, that an infant is less than human?

The flaw in Sandel's analogy stems from his unwillingness to draw a distinction between the substance of a being and its accidents. George and Lee note that we value (or at least should value) human beings for the kind of thing they are

---

[45] Baron de Montesquieu, *Spirit of the Laws* (1748), Thomas Nugent, trans. (London: G. Bell, 1914), Book 15, Ch. 5, 257.

[46] Robert P. George and Patrick Lee, Letter to the Editor, *The New England Journal of Medicine* (October 14, 2004), 1687.

whereas we "value oak trees because of certain accidental qualities."[47] Whether an oak tree is magnificent or grandiose has no bearing on what it is, but its size and age may matter quite a bit for how much we value it. With human beings it is (or at least should be) otherwise. Whether a person is young or old, black or white, large or small, comatose or lucid are accidental qualities unrelated to the kind of thing it is, and these qualities do not detract from a human being's inherent dignity. Here, again, our historical experience with slavery is illustrative. In a private fragment written in the early 1850s, Abraham Lincoln reconstructed a fictional conversation with a slave owner who defended the institution of slavery on the grounds that some accidental quality of the slaves justified their enslavement: "If A. can prove, however conclusively, that he may, of right, enslave B.," Lincoln asked,

– why may not B. snatch the same argument, and prove equally, that he may enslave A? –
  You say A. is white, and B. is black. It is *color*, then; the lighter, having the right to enslave the darker? Take care. By this rule, you are to be slave to the first man you meet, with a fairer skin than your own.
  You do not mean *color* exactly? – You mean the whites are *intellectually* the superiors of the blacks, and, therefore have the right to enslave them? Take care again. By this rule, you are to be slave to the first man you meet, with an intellect superior to your own.
  But, you say, it is a question of *interest*; and, if you can make it your *interest*, you have the right to enslave another. Very well. And if he can make it his interest, he has the right to enslave you.[48]

Lincoln's point, which he had an occasion to draw out in his political duel with Douglas, was that human status itself was sufficient to give someone a right to be free.

In the words of the Declaration, which Lincoln repeatedly invoked, all men are created equal and endowed by their Creator with certain unalienable rights. To deny this, as Douglas did, was, according to Lincoln, to go back to

[47] Ibid., 1687.
[48] Basler, ed., *Collected Works of Abraham Lincoln*, Vol. 2, 222–223.

the old argument for the "Divine Right of Kings." By the latter, the King is to do just as he pleases with his white subjects, being responsible to God alone. By the former the white man is to do just as he pleases with his black slaves, being responsible to God alone. The two things are precisely alike; and it is but natural that they should find similar arguments to sustain them.[49]

If, on the other hand, one wanted to embrace the egalitarian principles in the Declaration but still maintain the right of individual communities to decide the slavery question for themselves as a matter of principle, rather than political prudence, then the "all men" of the Declaration had to be understood in racially coded terms. And, indeed, Douglas did maintain that the Continental Congress "referred to the white race alone, and not to the African, when they declared all men to have been created equal."[50]

Even beyond this historical squabble about the intentions of the signers of the Declaration, Lincoln insisted that the heart of the problem was that Judge Douglas had "no very vivid impression that the negro is a human; and consequently [had] no idea that there can be any moral question in legislating about him."[51] The political and rhetorical difficulty in Lincoln's argument was that the moral principle that all human beings have certain rights simply by virtue of their humanity could not be logically or rationally demonstrated. "To deny these things," Lincoln said, summarizing his whole argument against slavery based on the principles of the Declaration, "is to deny our national axioms, or dogmas, at least; and it puts an end to all argument."[52] The reason it puts an end to all argument is simply because you cannot argue someone into accepting axioms. Rather, axioms provide the foundation for the argument. "One would start with great confidence that he could convince any sane child that the simpler propositions of Euclid are

[49] Ibid., Vol. 2, 278.
[50] Ibid., Vol. 2, 406.
[51] Ibid., Vol. 2, 281.
[52] Ibid., Vol. 2, 283.

true;" Lincoln wrote in a letter to Henry Pierce in 1859, "but nevertheless, he would fail, utterly, with one who should deny the definitions and axioms." With respect to slavery and republican government, Lincoln went on to suggest, "The principles of Jefferson are the definitions and axioms of a free society."[53] Partly because of Lincoln, and the rebirth of freedom he helped inaugurate, few in our country today would deny the axioms. Equality is our dogma, and we have a healthy disdain for slavery even as we continue to war against racial discrimination.

And yet abortion, when considered in merely descriptive terms, tests our true commitment to the equal dignity of all human beings. In a jarring essay published on the thirty-ninth anniversary of *Roe v. Wade*, law professor Michael Stokes Paulsen wrote simply that the landmark decision created "a constitutional right of some human beings to kill other human beings" – a description that was not intentionally "provocative, but simply direct – blunt about facts."[54] Indeed, there really is no debate (at least with respect to biology) about whether a new individual human life comes into existence at conception.[55] The right pronounced in *Roe*, then, can be none other than a right to destroy or terminate a unique, individual human being at an early stage of development. Rather than grappling with this fact, however, we often deal in euphemisms. In its *Roe* decision, for example, the Supreme Court repeatedly used the phrase "potential life" to refer to the unborn, and this common error – that something other than actual human life is involved in abortion – has skewed the abortion debate in America for the last four decades.

---

[53] Ibid.,Vol. 3, 375.
[54] Michael Stokes Paulsen, "The Unbearable Wrongness of Roe," *Public Discourse: Ethics, Law and the Common Good* (January 23, 2012), http://www.thepublic discourse.com/2012/01/4577.
[55] For a technical discussion about the humanity of the early embryo, see George and Tollefsen, *Embryo*, 144–173.

Consistency does make its own demands, however, and some proponents of abortion choice have been willing to rethink the standard political/legal euphemisms regarding fetal life. Shortly after Norma McCorvey's defection from the abortion rights movement, Naomi Wolf wrote an introspective piece for *The New Republic* chiding feminists for relying on a "political rhetoric in which the fetus means nothing."[56] The result of the rhetorical strategy of dehumanizing the unborn was that abortion rights activists became entangled in "a series of self-delusions, fibs and evasions" – what she later called a "lexicon of dehumanization."[57] Recognizing that the unborn are both human beings and persons, Wolf simply claimed that "Sometimes the mother must be able to decide that the fetus, in its full humanity, must die."[58] It was bracing candor, but Wolf ultimately sought solace in a secularized paradigm of sin and salvation, which emphasized both a woman's right to choose death for her child and her correlative obligation to seek absolution through "acts of redemption."[59] In an allusion to the biblical concept of substitutionary atonement, Wolf went so far as to characterize the spilling of blood in an abortion procedure as salvific:

> By resisting a moral framework in which to view abortion we who are pro-abortion-rights leave the doctors in the front lines, with blood on their hands: the blood of the repeat abortions – at least 43 percent of the total; the suburban summer country-club rite-of-passage abortions; the "I don't know what came over me, it was such good Chardonnay" abortions; as well as the blood of the desperate and the unpreventable and accidental and the medically necessary and the violently conceived abortions. This is blood that the doctors and clinic workers often see clearly, and that they heroically rinse and cause to flow and rinse again. And they take all our sins, the pro-choice as well as the pro-life among us, upon themselves.[60]

[56] Naomi Wolf, "Our Bodies, Our Souls," *The New Republic* (October 16, 1995), 26.
[57] Ibid., 26.
[58] Ibid., 33.
[59] Ibid., 35.
[60] Ibid., 35. Cf. Isaiah 53 and Hebrews 9:24–26.

Wolf's emphasis on a moral framework for abortion rights and her invocation of a quasi-theological hope for redemption through the ritual bloodletting and sacrifice of the young in the abortion procedure brings the discussion full circle – to the idea of public reason and the quest for a shared moral framework in which to conduct our public debate.

But even if we, as a society, were to reluctantly dispense with the euphemisms, we would remain deeply divided on the moral and political questions involving human beings at this stage of development – Are they moral persons? If so, does it matter? Could there nevertheless be a constitutional right to choose their death? A common answer to these questions is that unborn human beings are not persons, and personhood, in turn, is a concept that is politically constructed. But if one tugs at the threads in this line of reasoning, the entire apparatus supporting the theory of natural rights rooted in a transcendent moral law begins to unravel, and as these theoretical foundations unravel, so, too, do the underlying principles of democracy and the rule of law. As Lewis maintained, the

> very idea of freedom presupposes some objective moral law which overarches rulers and ruled alike. Subjectivism about values is eternally incompatible with democracy. We and our rulers are of one kind only so long as we are subject to one law. But if there is no Law of Nature, the ethos of any society is the creation of its rulers, educators and conditioners; and every creator stands above and outside his creation.[61]

This may seem hyperbolic, but it is not. If our beginning axiom, our foundational principle, is that all human beings are the bearers of basic rights simply by virtue of the kind of thing they are, we betray that principle by treating some biological human beings as though they were not human.

But if we doubt whether there is an objective, empirical standard of "what constitutes a human being, the decision," as Hadley Arkes notes, "will be left in the hands then of

[61] Lewis, "The Poison of Subjectivism," 81.

people with political power. And when they flex their power, in reaching a judgment, that judgment will be tested by no standard of right or wrong *apart from power itself.*" To bring the point back to the issues of slavery and abortion: There simply is no neutral ground with respect to the question of who counts as a full person or human being in our political order. Yet "the moves are all familiar to us," Arkes observes,

and we have heard them, in different forms, over the years: "Are those black people, held in slavery, really human beings, or are they creatures falling somewhere between human beings and animals? And those creatures in the womb – they are conceived by human beings, but does that mean that they are human at all times? Can we not rid ourselves of them if they strain our interests, just as we may rid ourselves of certain animals, with discomfort, perhaps, but without moral strain? But who is to say?"[62]

And so we end, where we began, with the prevalent comparisons between slavery and abortion, and the parallels between these issues on deep principles of constitutionalism. The central question, involving the deepest principles, is simply, who counts as a member of our political and moral community?

---

[62] Hadley Arkes, *Natural Rights and the Right to Choose* (New York: Cambridge University Press, 2002), 5 (emphasis in original).

# 7

# Personhood and the Ethics of Life

The central question in the abortion debates, as Richard John Neuhaus long contended, is simply, "Who belongs to the community for which we accept common responsibility?"[1] For many of the most influential voices in the academic debate about the ethics and legality of abortion, the answer to this question hinges on some conception of personhood. "Beginning in the ancient world," John Rawls noted, "the concept of the person has been understood, in both philosophy and law, as the concept of someone who can take part in, or who can play a role in, social life, and hence exercise and respect its various rights and duties."[2] A person is a member of the political and social community, whereas a non-person stands outside of that community and can neither claim its rights nor be subject to its obligations.

In his *Dred Scott* opinion, Roger Taney made such a conception of personhood central to the question of whether African slaves and their descendants could ever claim American citizenship, and Taney's suggestion that

---

[1] Richard John Neuhaus, "The End of Abortion and the Meaning of 'Christian America,'" *First Things* (June/July 2001), 67.

[2] John Rawls, *Political Liberalism*, expanded edition (New York: Columbia University Press, 2005 [1993]), 18.

African slaves formed no part of "the people" for whom the Constitution was written was a historical claim about conventional rights and duties. For "more than a century," Taney maintained, slaves were "regarded as beings of an inferior order ... and so far inferior that they had no rights which the white man was bound to respect." Having no legal rights, the slave was "bought and sold, and treated as an ordinary article of merchandise and traffic whenever a profit could be made by it."[3] Although Taney's simplistic reading of history was challenged by the dissenting opinions of Benjamin Curtis and John McLean, it was of course true that slaves *were* treated as property, and therefore something less than full persons, throughout much of the eighteenth and nineteenth centuries. The inconsistency of slavery with the underlying principles of American government led many abolitionists to conclude that slavery, if not arrested, would eventually destroy the "institutions of the country" and mark "the white man's liberty ... for the same grave as the black man's."[4] Abortion creates a similar tension between ideals and practice, and, like slavery, abortion's perpetual existence and political protection threaten to erode the anchoring principles of republican government.

Unsurprisingly, leading voices in the pro-life movement have long drawn lessons from the political history of abolitionism, and pro-life organizations often turn to the legacies of William Wilberforce and Abraham Lincoln when crafting political strategies designed to put abortion on a course toward ultimate extinction.[5] The historical success of abolitionism, which once seemed impractical and hopeless, has

---

[3] *Dred Scott v. Sandford* 60 U.S. 393, 404–5 (Taney, J.).

[4] John W. Blassingame, ed., *The Frederick Douglass Papers Series One: Speeches, Debates, and Interviews*, 5 vols. (New Haven, CT: Yale University Press, 1985), Vol. 3, 169.

[5] See, for example, Clarke D. Forsythe, *Politics for the Greatest Good: The Case for Prudence in the Public Square* (Downers Grove, IL: InterVarsity Press, 2009). See also Pennsylvania Governor Robert Casey's speech on the steps of the courthouse in St. Louis (a deliberate allusion to *Dred Scott*), reprinted as "Law Without Honor," *Human Life Review* 19, no. 2 (Spring 1993), 54–64.

also imbued pro-life forces with a sense of optimism in the face of seemingly implacable political opposition. "What all Americans need to understand," Neuhaus admonished, "is that pro-life activists typically do believe that their children or their children's children will live in a world in which people will look back upon the abortion license with the same abhorrence with which we today look back upon slavery. They will, it is expected, shake their heads in horrified wonder at the fact that it was once legal and socially acceptable to kill children at will."[6]

There is, however, nothing inevitable about culture or politics, and there are no guarantees that future generations will come to regard abortion as the historical artifact of a barbaric past. A plausible alternative future was recently outlined in a high-profile academic article about the ethics of infanticide. "Both a fetus and a newborn are human beings," Alberto Giubilini and Fransesca Minerva concluded in the pages of the international *Journal of Medical Ethics*, "but neither is a 'person' in the sense of 'subject of a moral right to life.'"[7] The authors' argument is that there are no morally relevant differences between an about-to-be-born baby and a newborn that would distinguish the ethics of late-term abortion from infanticide. Although this could be pushed in one of two directions, Giubilini and Minerva suggest that "when circumstances occur *after birth* such that they would have justified abortion, what we call *after-birth abortion* should be permissible."[8]

The authors readily acknowledge that their argument makes the humanity of the newborn irrelevant. "Merely being human," they contend, "is not in itself a reason for ascribing someone a right to life."[9] The crucial question for

[6] Neuhaus, "The End of Abortion," 71.
[7] Alberto Giubilini and Fransesca Minerva, "After-Birth Abortion: Why Should the Baby Live?" *Journal of Medical Ethics* (2012) [doi:10/1136/medethics-2011-100411], 2.
[8] Ibid., 2.
[9] Ibid.

the authors is whether a newborn is a "person," defined as "an individual who is capable of attributing to her own existence some (at least) basic value such that being deprived of this existence represents a loss to her."[10] Since personhood so defined is a function of mental development, there can be no hard and fast rule about when, if ever, a human being becomes a person. Relatedly, some non-human animals would be persons under this definition, even as some humans are considered non-persons.

## PERSONHOOD AND POLITICAL LIBERALISM

Although the *Journal of Medical Ethics* article defending so-called after-birth abortion was intentionally provocative, there was nothing truly original in it. Other prominent ethicists have defended the practice of infanticide, and liberal theorists who stop short of defending after-birth abortions often make similar distinctions between human beings and moral persons. Rawls, for example, began his theory of "justice as fairness" by constructing a political conception of persons as "free and equal" members of a mutually beneficial system of social cooperation over time. In order to engage in such social cooperation, Rawls posited, a human being must have both a capacity for a sense of justice and a capacity for a conception of the good. Possessing these two "moral powers" is, in turn, all that is implied by "moral personality" in Rawls's influential political theory.[11]

Rawls's conception of personhood, defined in this way, begs the question of when personhood begins. A person, Rawls asserted,

> is someone who can be a citizen, that is, a normal and fully cooperating member of society over a complete life. We add the phrase "over a complete life" because society is viewed not only as closed (§2.1) but as a more or less complete and self-sufficient

[10] Ibid.
[11] See Rawls, *Political Liberalism* (New York: Columbia University Press, 2005), 1§3 (pp. 15–22) and 1§5 (pp. 29–35).

scheme of cooperation, making room within itself for all the neces-
sities and activities of life, from birth until death.

The phrase "over a complete life" is crucial to the initial
question of who counts as a member of our community.
When does our complete life begin, and why does personhood commence at birth? Do unborn children not also have
a capacity for a sense of justice and a conception of the
good? Surely the capacity does not have to be actualized or
immediately exercisable, for then we could not be persons
"over a complete life" – from birth until death – as Rawls
insisted we are, since newborns (and older children) are
equally unable to exercise these capacities.[12]

A clue to Rawls's own thinking on how to conceptualize
abortion was provided in a pair of footnotes in *Political
Liberalism*. In an early edition, Rawls considered the types
of arguments that could be brought to bear on the "troubled
question of abortion." For the purposes of illustrating how
his theory of public reason would operate in practice, Rawls
considered "the question in terms of these three important
political values: the due respect for human life, the orderly
reproduction of political society over time, including the
family in some form, and finally the equality of women as
equal citizens." "Now I believe," Rawls wrote,

> any reasonable balance of these three values will give a woman a
> duly qualified right to decide whether or not to end her pregnancy
> during the first trimester. The reason for this is that at this early
> stage of pregnancy the political value of the equality of women is
> overriding, and this right is required to give it substance and force.
> Other political values, if tallied in, would not, I think, affect this
> conclusion. A reasonable balance may allow her such a right
> beyond this, at least in certain circumstances. However, I do not
> discuss the question in general here, as I simply want to illustrate
> the point of the text by saying that any comprehensive doctrine that
> leads to a balance of political values excluding that duly qualified
> right in the first trimester is to that extent unreasonable; and
> depending on the details of its formulation, it may also be cruel

[12] Of our "closed society," Rawls maintained that we "enter it only by birth and
leave it only by death." See *Political Liberalism*, 18.

and oppressive; for example if it denied the right altogether except in the case of rape or incest.[13]

In structuring his comments this way, Rawls assumed answers to some very weighty questions: What regard *is* due to human life, and when exactly *does* human life begin? What does our interest in societal reproduction mean for human beings that *already* exist? Relatedly, when did a woman, possessed of equal rights, come into possession of her rights? When she was an unborn child in the second trimester? When she was born? Or at some later stage of development?

To be fair, Rawls later clarified that he was expressing an opinion on the matter rather than making an argument for the reasonableness of his opinion. Nonetheless, he suggested that such an argument could be "developed at public reason," and he specifically offered a *Boston Review* essay written by Judith Jarvis Thomson as one such example. Thomson's essay was written on the heels of the Supreme Court's reaffirmation of *Roe* in *Planned Parenthood* v. *Casey* (1992), and it came during a time of heightened violence committed by anti-abortion militants. Perhaps the political (rather than philosophical) nature of her argument explains its appeal to Rawls, since he insisted that Thomson's essay offered a reasonable argument on a matter of basic justice that fell within the bounds of public reason.

In the essay Thomson suggested that the national abortion debate was at a standstill precisely because reasonable people disagreed about the moral status of the fetus. In light of the fact of reasonable disagreement, Thomson argued that women should be free to choose abortion, because any restriction on the abortion liberty could not "be justified *to* them" and would therefore be "nothing but an exercise of force."[14] This is, of course, similar to Rawls's own suggestion that

---

[13] Rawls, *Political Liberalism*, 243–244 n. 32.
[14] Judith Jarvis Thomson, "Abortion," *Boston Review* (Summer 1995), http://bostonreview.net/BR20.3/thomson.html.

in political debate we should give reasons that are found in an overlapping consensus among reasonable doctrines and, in this way, offer other citizens reasons they can accept on their own terms. All of this brings the inquiry back to the question we started with: Who counts as a person and as a member of the community for which we have common concern? Once again, the slavery analogy works as a powerful heuristic device, for if we make the same argument about slavery (and the same argument *was* made about slavery), the fallacy in the reasoning is more evident.

The basic premise of Stephen Douglas's popular sovereignty argument was that men are capable of governing themselves and should be allowed to do so. But to say that A should be allowed to enslave B as a matter of self-government presumes that B does not have an equal right of self-government. And if self-government is a natural right – that is, one possessed by virtue of being human – then enslaving someone else as a matter of self-government is to treat him as devoid of natural rights and therefore less than human. Since Douglas's argument assumed an answer to the very thing people disagreed about (i.e., the full humanity of one race of people), Lincoln repeatedly claimed, it could not truly be premised on the grounds of neutrality between competing views.

And so it is with abortion. The argument that abortion should be protected precisely because reasonable people disagree about the morality of intentionally killing the unborn implicitly assumes either that the unborn are not fully human or that some humans are less than full moral persons. On the other hand, the "traditional condemnation of therapeutic abortion," as John Finnis noted in 1973, rests "on the basis that mother and child are *equally* persons in whom the value of human life is to be realized (or the 'right to life' respected) and not directly attacked."[15] That idea, in

---

[15] John Finnis, "The Rights and Wrongs of Abortion: A Reply to Judith Thomson," *Philosophy & Public Affairs* 2, no. 2 (1973), 132.

turn, rests on the premise that "the baby, still not born, is a man in the same degree and for the same reason as the mother."[16] Anyone who holds these two premises will not be persuaded by the argument that it is wrong in principle to protect the unborn from violence at the hands of those who do not recognize its humanity, any more than a committed nineteenth-century abolitionist would have been persuaded to abandon the cause of abolition simply because reasonable and decent slaveholders disagreed about the morality of slavery.

Of course there may have been good prudential reasons to compromise with slavery and to craft incremental political strategies designed to eliminate it over time, but that is different than protecting slavery as a legitimate matter of private choice. Similarly, there may be good reasons to work for incremental restrictions on abortion and to strike political compromises when necessary, but these prudential considerations are separate from the root question of whether the unborn are moral persons whom it would be wrong to kill. For these reasons Rawls' turn to politics instead of metaphysics is unhelpful, since the principled political disagreement is at root metaphysical. It is *meta*physical because the answer to the physical question of whether the unborn are human beings is straightforward and uncontroversial; in a strictly biological sense, they are. But defenders of abortion choice often appeal to a distinction between human beings and human persons in order to mark off one segment of humanity as something less than full moral persons.

The point of such distinctions, as Robert Wertheimer has observed, is to separate analytically the realm of values from the realm of facts.[17] Although we can, through empirical observation, come to some agreement about when a

---

[16] *Encyclical Letter of Pope Pius XII on Christian Marriage* (St. Paul Editions: Boston, n.d.). Cited in Finnis, "The Rights and Wrongs of Abortion," 132–3 n. 26.
[17] Roger Wertheimer, "Understanding the Abortion Argument," *Philosophy & Public Affairs* 1, no. 1 (1971), 78.

new member of our species comes into existence, the debate about personhood shifts the discussion from the realm of "is" to the realm of "ought." In the process, we move from the domain of speculative reason to the realm of practical reason, since the simple observation that X is a member of the species *Homo sapiens* does not tell us anything about why or when X becomes the kind of thing that it would be morally wrong to kill. And as the myriad scholarly defenses of infanticide demonstrate, the value-laden debate about personhood – that is, about when human beings attain a certain moral status – has implications that travel far beyond the point of birth.

## INFANTICIDE AND HUMAN PERSONS

The various parallels and analogies between slavery and abortion became a prominent feature of the academic debate in the early 1970s, and many of these issues were considered in connection with the ethics of killing newborns. While the Supreme Court was preparing for oral re-argument in *Roe v. Wade*, Michael Tooley broached the issue of infanticide in the pages of *Philosophy & Public Affairs*. "One reason the question of the morality of infanticide is worth examining," Tooley wrote, "is that it seems very difficult to formulate a completely satisfactory liberal position on abortion without coming to grips with infanticide."[18] The difficulty for the defender of abortion is delineating some non-arbitrary criterion to distinguish the licit killing of a human being at one point on a developmental continuum from the illicit killing of the same being at some other point. This delicate task requires one to "be very clear about what makes something a person, and what gives something a right to life."[19] In Tooley's analytical framework, personhood and the right not to be killed

---

[18] Michael Tooley, "Abortion and Infanticide," *Philosophy & Public Affairs* 2, no. 1 (1972), 37–38.
[19] Ibid., 38.

are two sides of the same coin. A moral person, he asserted, is by definition someone who "has a (serious) moral right to life."[20]

Still, Tooley insisted that not all human beings are moral persons, and he suggested that the distinction between a human being and a moral person was an essential, but neglected, part of the case for abortion choice. In many of the debates in the 1960s and early 1970s, Tooley noted, there had "been a tendency" in "discussion of abortion to use 'person' and 'human being' interchangeably.'" Indeed, as one philosopher noted, "the expressions 'a human life,' 'a human being,' 'a person' are virtually interchangeable in this context."[21] Tooley, however, insisted that the common interchangeable use of "person" and "human being" in the debates about the legalization of abortion was "unfortunate" because it tended "to lend covert support to antiabortionist positions." If the debate was simply about whether a fetus was a human being, then the anti-abortion argument was clearly stronger, since the unborn are, in fact, human beings.

The virtue of (a) drawing a sharp distinction between human beings and moral persons and (b) focusing the debate on the latter question, Tooley argued, was that it removed the "temptation to suppose that the disagreement must be a factual one."[22] But lurking in the background, again, was the unique American experience with slavery. "The parallels with the abortion controversy are palpable," Wertheimer claimed in the same journal a year before Tooley's article about infanticide.[23] And although Wertheimer remained agnostic about the morality of abortion, he nonetheless claimed that the moral questions at stake in the controversies over slavery and abortion were

---

[20] Ibid.
[21] Wertheimer, "Understanding the Abortion Argument," 69. Cited in Tooley, "Abortion and Infanticide," 41.
[22] Tooley, "Abortion and Infanticide," 41.
[23] Wertheimer, "Understanding the Abortion Argument," 84.

at base factual questions.[24] When "disagreement develops from differing responses to the same data," Wertheimer noted,

> the issue is still a factual one and not a matter of taste. It is not that one party prefers or approves of or has a favorable attitude or emotion toward some property, while the other party does not. Our response concerns what the thing is, not whether we like it or whether it is good. And when I say I don't *care* about the color of a man's skin, that it's not *important* to me, I am saying something quite different than when I say I don't care about the color of a woman's hair. I am saying that this property cannot be used to justify discriminatory behavior or social arrangements. It cannot be so used because it is irrelevant; neither black skin nor white skin is, in and of itself, of any value. Skin color has no logical relation to the question of how to treat a man. The slaveholder's response is not that white skin is of intrinsic value. Rather, he replies that people with naturally black skin are niggers, and that is an inferior kind of creature. So too, the liberal does not claim that infants possess some intrinsically valuable attribute lacked by prenatal children. Rather, he says that a prenatal child is a fetus, not a human being.[25]

Wertheimer thus called Tooley's fact–value distinction into question. The factual question was inseparable from the moral question, and if "one insists on using that raggy fact-value distinction," he declared, then "one ought to say that the dispute is over a matter of fact in the sense in which it is a fact that the Negro slaves were human beings."[26]

Tooley therefore began his analysis "by considering the similarity a number of people have noted between the issue of abortion and the issue of Negro slavery."[27] "The question here," Tooley asserted,

> is why it should be more difficult to decide why abortion and infanticide are acceptable than it was to decide whether slavery was acceptable. The answer seems to be that in the case of slavery there are moral principles of a quite uncontroversial sort that settle the issue. Thus most people would agree to some such principle as the following: No organism that has experiences, that is capable of thought and

[24] On Wertheimer's agnosticism, see ibid., 88.
[25] Ibid., 85.
[26] Ibid., 78.
[27] Ibid., 43.

of using language, and that has harmed no one, should be made a slave. In the case of abortion, on the other hand, conditions that are generally agreed to be sufficient grounds for ascribing a right to life to something do not suffice to settle the issue.[28]

The difficulty with Tooley's response is that reasonable slaveholders would have disagreed with the very moral principles he took to be uncontroversial, and it makes little sense to appeal to a consensus in twentieth-century American culture to say why slavery was morally "unacceptable" in the nineteenth century.

Beyond the issue of slavery, Tooley's definition of personhood also brought to the table a challenge for the issue of abortion. An organism possesses a serious right to life, Tooley suggested, "if it possesses the concept of a self as a continuing subject of experiences and other mental states, and believes that it is itself such a continuing entity."[29] Although this working definition of moral personhood allowed Tooley to make a clear distinction between what is involved in abortion and what is involved in the enslavement of a self-conscious adult, it did not sharply distinguish abortion from infanticide. Because "a newborn does not possess the concept of a continuing self," Tooley asserted, "infanticide during a time interval shortly after birth must be morally acceptable."[30] Tooley was one of the first philosophers to defend the morality of infanticide in a professional journal, but the argument is now commonplace. As Peter Singer writes in the most recent edition of his widely used textbook on ethics,

the fact that a being is a human being, in the sense of a member of the species *Homo sapiens*, is not relevant to the wrongness of killing it; instead, characteristics like rationality, autonomy, and self-awareness make a difference. Infants lack these characteristics. Killing them, therefore, cannot be equated with killing normal human beings, or any other self-aware beings.[31]

---

[28] Ibid., 42.
[29] Ibid., 44.
[30] Ibid., 63.
[31] Peter Singer, *Practical Ethics*, 3rd ed. (New York: Cambridge University Press, 2011), 160–61.

"No infant – disabled or not –" Singer claims, "has as strong an intrinsic claim to life as beings capable of seeing themselves as distinct entities existing over time."[32] Recent defenses of infanticide, including the *Medical Ethics* article by Giubilini and Minerva, further develop the rationale for infanticide by specifying criteria to distinguish between human beings and human persons.

## PERFORMANCE V. ENDOWMENT

Whether implicit or explicit, all attempts to distinguish human persons from human beings end up grading humanity into various levels of moral value or worth. A human person is a human being who has certain performance-based attributes, for example, self-consciousness or some specified level of cognitive functioning. As a result, the traditional egalitarian ethic that emphasizes the moral equality of all human beings is called into question, since all human beings do not equally share the defining attributes of personhood (whatever they happen to be). "It is hard to avoid the sense that our egalitarian commitments rest on distressingly insecure foundations," philosopher Jeff McMahan conceded in a recent *Journal of Ethics* article provocatively titled "Challenges to Human Equality."[33] McMahan had in mind two central problems that bedevil all performance-based theories of moral personhood: In each account, it is difficult to (1) say why human beings should be afforded a higher moral status than non-human animals with a similar level of cognitive functioning and (2) why human beings with different levels of cognitive functioning should be afforded the same moral status. The conclusion that many ethicists have come to is that these two prongs of our liberal egalitarian commitments are philosophically untenable. And so, as is often the case, abortion (along with infanticide)

---

[32] Ibid.
[33] Jeff McMahan, "Challenges to Human Equality," *The Journal of Ethics* 12, no. 1 (2008), 104.

is defended as a morally acceptable choice while other aspects of our traditional distinction between human beings and non-human animals is called into question. "If I am right that there is nothing in or invariably correlated with membership in the human species that can be the basis of our moral equality," McMahan contended, "then whatever the criterion of equal moral status is – and particularly if it is connected with psychological capacity – either some human beings are not our moral equals or some animals are."[34]

In academic philosophy, the chief rival to the performance-based conception of moral personhood espoused by Tooley, Singer, McMahan, and others is simply the view that all human beings are equal moral persons by virtue of their status as human beings. At bottom, these are our only two options: Either human beings become moral persons after functioning in a particular way or reaching a certain point of psychological development (and cease to be moral persons when they stop functioning in a particular way or degenerate back to a certain level of cognition), or all human beings just are moral persons. The latter account, Christopher Kaczor notes, "holds that each human being has inherent, moral worth simply by virtue of the kind of being it is." Humans, in other words, are "beings with endowments that orient them towards moral values, such as rationality, autonomy, and respect" and such beings "thereby merit inclusion as members of the moral community."[35] Although a human being's rational abilities may be incipient or temporarily impaired or permanently damaged, he or she remains the kind of being that is by nature a moral person. And so the reply to the defender of infanticide is simply that "infants do not become persons when they start thinking they are persons. Thinking is just one stage of personal development, made possible by the capacity to do so."[36]

---

[34] Ibid., 93.

[35] Christopher Kaczor, *The Ethics of Abortion: Women's Rights, Human Life, and the Question of Justice* (New York: Routledge, 2011), 93.

[36] John F. Kavanaugh, S.J., *Who Counts as Persons? Human Identity and the Ethics of Killing* (Washington, DC: Georgetown University Press, 2001), 67.

Central to the endowment account is a rejection of the body–self dualism that underwrites the philosophical distinction between human beings and moral persons.[37] According to the endowment view, we are not (as is often suggested) persons who inhabit a body, but embodied persons. There is thus a unity in our animal and personal existence. To be a human animal at any age or stage of development is to be a person. That is to say, being human means having "a nature which includes the basic natural capacities for conceptual thought and free choice."[38] Of course, the performance account

> denies this and holds that a being is to be accorded respect, if and only if, the being functions in a given way. There are numerous and conflicting accounts of what this function is, but some of the proposed candidates include: self-awareness, rationality, sentience, desirability, ethnicity, economic productivity, gender, nationality, native language, beauty, age, health, religion, race, ethnicity, fertility, birth, and national origin.[39]

Each of these characteristics has seemed plausible at various times and in various places, but "when considered in light of history it seems apparent that *every single time* the performance view has been chosen over the endowment view, gross moral mistakes were made."[40] "*Every* previous division of humankind," Kaczor contends, "was divided into two classes by some version of performance evaluation in which one half was permitted to dispose of the other at will – men exploiting women, whites selling blacks, the young dispatching the old, the rich utilizing the poor, the healthy overpowering the sickly – and are nearly universally recognized as evil."[41]

---

[37] See, generally, Robert P. George and Patrick Lee, *Body-Self Dualism in Contemporary Ethics and Politics* (Cambridge: Cambridge University Press, 2008).
[38] George and Lee, *Body-Self Dualism*, 51.
[39] Kaczor, *The Ethics of Abortion*, 93.
[40] Ibid., 102.
[41] Ibid., 102.

This historical perspective is, in part, why American opponents of abortion appeal so frequently to the history and legacy of slavery. Although the morality of slavery was in sharp dispute in our own country just a century and a half ago, there is now a wide consensus that race-based chattel slavery was a grave moral evil because it arbitrarily excluded some human persons from the moral community and damaged those persons by treating them as consumable property. In this, the contemporary view is certainly a corrective to the pernicious racial theories of the nineteenth century. As C. S. Lewis contended, in the voice of the satirical devil Screwtape, "where learning makes a free commerce between the ages there is always the danger that the characteristic errors of one may by corrected by the characteristic truths of another."[42] Lewis' observation cuts two ways, and the frequent analogies between abortion and slavery are often drawn to suggest that our modern culture may have something to learn from previous generations. In this vein, the abortion-related articles published in medical journals in the nineteenth century are particularly good correctives for our own errors, since the medical community did not entertain a false and ad hoc dualism between human beings and human persons. When discussing the ethics of abortion, the relevant factual consideration for nineteenth-century physicians and jurists was when a distinct human being came into existence. The reigning ethical paradigm was one that saw human beings as embodied persons attaining a high moral status precisely because of the kind of thing a human being is.

The physicians thus approached the issue with a confidence and moral clarity that is jarring to our modern sensibilities. Walter Channing, the first Professor of Obstetrics and Medical Jurisprudence at Harvard College and the brother of abolitionist William Ellery Channing, referred to abortion simply as "unborn-child-killing" and distinguished criminal

---

[42] C. S. Lewis, *The Complete C. S. Lewis Signature Classics* (New York: HarperCollins, 2002), 265.

abortion from natural miscarriage by referring to the former as abortion "produced by violence."[43] In a lecture on medical jurisprudence reprinted in Edwin Hale's *Systematic Treatise on Abortion* (1866), Professor A. E. Small thought it proper to consider the "heinousness" of abortion "in light of the moral law, which regards the willful killing of a human being, at any stage of its existence, as nothing short of murder."[44] This conclusion, Small suggested, followed simply from "the fact that foetal life is human life, distinct from that of the mother's, and dependent upon an organization as distinct from that of the mother's as if it were entirely liberated from its resting place in her womb."[45] Once a new human being came into existence, Small asserted, "the inalienable rights of a human life are implied."[46] Similar characterizations of abortion were ubiquitous in medical journals of the mid- and late nineteenth century. Abortion was described as a "crime against life,"[47] "child-murder,"[48] "the willful destruction of ante-natal human life,"[49] a sin "against God and man,"[50] and a great "holocaust."[51]

The latter characterization came from Mary A. Dixon-Jones, a prolific nineteenth-century medical researcher,

[43] Walter Channing, "Effects of Criminal Abortion," *Boston Medical and Surgical Journal* LX, no. 7 (March 17, 1859), 135; 139.

[44] A. E. Small, "Criminal Abortion," Lecture at Hahnemann Medical College (December 1864). Reprinted in Edwin Hale, *Treatise on Criminal Abortion* (Chicago: C. S. Halsey, 1866), 313.

[45] Ibid., 313.

[46] Ibid., 317.

[47] Horatio Robinson Storer, *Why Not? A Book for Every Woman* (Boston: Lee and Shepard, 1866), 15.

[48] Homer Hitchcock, "Report on Criminal Abortion," *Fourth Annual Report of the Secretary of the State Board of Health of the State of Michigan* (Lansing, MI: W. S. George & Co., 1876), 58.

[49] Andrew Nebinger, "Criminal Abortion: Its Extent and Prevention," *Transactions of the Medical Society of the State of Pennsylvania at its Twenty-Seventh Annual Session*, XI, Part I (Philadelphia, 1876), 119.

[50] M. M. Eaton, "Four and A-Half Inches of Whalebone in the Uterus. – Abortion – Narrow Escape from Death," *Chicago Medical Examiner* IX, no. 4 (April 1868), 218.

[51] Mary A. Dixon-Jones, "Criminal Abortion. Its Evils and Its Sad Consequences," *Medical Record* XLVI, no. 1 (July 7, 1894), 10.

surgeon, and pathologist.[52] The reason for abortion in many instances, Dixon-Jones claimed, was ignorance. Women (and men) seeking to end a pregnancy did "not sufficiently know the great mysteries and beauties of life, that from the moment of conception a child begins to live, that as soon as there is a combination of the two elements, it is a human being."[53] But if they had a sufficient appreciation for the fact that the developing young at the earliest stage of pregnancy "is then a human being," they would perceive that abortion "is a most cruel warfare, a most unfair battle, more cowardly than the midnight assassin, or he who puts the dagger in the heart of the unsuspecting."[54] Particularly troubling to her were the unprincipled rationales that were occasionally put forward to justify abortion. In the *New York Gynecological Journal*, Dixon-Jones noted, a doctor named C. H. Harris openly opined "that the world would be better if abortion were done oftener."[55] This, however, was a minority sentiment in the medical community, and the journal itself "heartily reprobate[d] the article by Dr. Harris, not merely because [the journal was] opposed on principle to the practices which he advocates but equally because his advocacy of them is illogical, and founded upon arguments of expediency which appeal to self interest of the lower and more dangerous kind."[56]

The unprincipled nature of the argument for unfettered abortion choice troubled Dixon-Jones. Abortion, "when life is endangered, may be judicious;" she claimed,

> but, in general, if one's individual judgment may decide whether it is best for a child in utero to live, may not the same individual judgment decide whether it is expedient for a boy or girl of five or

[52] For a biographical sketch of Dixon-Jones published by the National Institutes of Health, see http://www.nlm.nih.gov/changingthefaceofmedicine/physicians/biography_176.html.

[53] Dixon-Jones, "Criminal Abortion," 10.

[54] Ibid., 11.

[55] C. H. Harris, "Special Operation for Abortion," *New York Gynecological Journal* (September, 1892), 842. Cited in Dixon-Jones, "Criminal Abortion," 15.

[56] Ibid., 845. Cited in Dixon-Jones, "Criminal Abortion," 15 n. 3.

ten years of age to live. If, in one's private judgment, a human being in utero may be destroyed, with equal right may we not destroy a human being at any age of existence? May we not, at any time, decide whether anyone's life is useful or to the advantage of him or herself and to the community? Is not this a most dangerous doctrine? Could a more cruel despotism exist? A physician has no more right to destroy a human foetus, because he imagines it, in future years, may be sickly, than he has a right to destroy the delicate baby, because it possibly may have before it years of invalidism.[57]

Of course, what Dixon-Jones took to be uncontroversial – that at least a baby *after birth* should be protected against violence – is precisely what our age has come to question. And while Dixon-Jones considered the case of a child who may suffer from years of invalidism, the modern defenses of infanticide make no such qualifications. Singer concedes that the "*intrinsic* wrongness of killing the late fetus and the *intrinsic* wrongness of killing the newborn infant are not markedly different," and he goes on to countenance infanticide "when those closest to the child do not want it to live."[58] Similarly, Giubilini and Minerva argue that parents should be allowed to kill a healthy born child even if there are people willing to adopt the child.[59] Jeff McMahan concludes that it is morally permissible to intentionally kill a healthy orphaned newborn in order to harvest his or her organs for donation to older (self-aware) children awaiting transplants.[60] Each of these arguments flows from various theories of personhood that divorce moral status from human status.

## THE COLLAPSE OF THE WESTERN ETHIC

As Singer noted in 1994, "the traditional western ethic has collapsed" and we have entered "a period of transition in

---

[57] Dixon-Jones, "Criminal Abortion," 16.
[58] Singer, *Practical Ethics*, 154.
[59] Giubilini and Minerva, "After-birth Abortion: Why Should the Baby Live?" 3.
[60] Jeff McMahan, *The Ethics of Killing: Problems at the Margins of Life* (New York: Oxford University Press, 2008), 22.

our attitudes about the sanctity of life."[61] Two years before Singer announced the "collapse of our traditional values," some of the implications of our changing ethics were on display in the Supreme Court's plurality opinion in *Planned Parenthood* v. *Casey*. "At the heart of liberty," three Reagan/Bush appointees wrote, "is the right to define one's own concept of existence, of meaning, of the universe, and of the mystery of human life. Beliefs about these matters could not define the attributes of personhood were they formed under compulsion of the State."[62] This well-known line – which Justice Scalia later mocked as the "famed-sweet-mystery-of-life passage"[63] – claimed that each individual was at liberty to define for herself both the "mystery of human life" and the attributes that make a human being a person. But in the context of the case, this right to define human life and fix the attributes of person-hood meant the right of one (adult) human being to decide whether another (prenatal) human being is a person; and the practical implication was that the Constitution secures a right privately to destroy or terminate non-persons. The new constitutional right defended by the Court thus brought back the question asked by Mary Dixon-Jones at the close of the nineteenth century: "If, in one's private judgment, a human being in utero may be destroyed, with equal right may we not destroy a human being at any age of existence?"[64] The confused formula in *Casey* is unhelpful in answering this question, since it makes the personhood of one human being depend on the idiosyncratic and subjective definition of another human being – a position that descends into nihilism if taken seriously.

[61] Peter Singer, *Rethinking Life and Death: The Collapse of Our Traditional Ethics* (New York: St. Martin's, 1995), 1.

[62] *Planned Parenthood* v. *Casey* 505 U.S. 833, 851 (1992) (O'Connor, Kennedy, and Souter, JJ.).

[63] *Lawrence* v. *Texas* 539 U.S. 538, 588 (2003) (Scalia, J., dissenting).

[64] Jones, "Criminal Abortion," 16.

A coherent defense of abortion requires at least an initial distinction between (and thus fixed definition of) human beings and human persons. But to distinguish human persons from human non-persons is simply to offer a different variation of the same tautology: Persons are those human beings who have moral rights because they have attribute Y, and nonpersons are those human beings who do not have moral rights because they lack attribute Y. The relevant attribute, however, is simply posited by people with power. The fundamental disagreement splitting the two sides in the current debate is thus whether "personhood is an ontological reality or a social construction."[65] Against the new ethics of killing, which relies on moral gradations of humanity and rejects the notion of natural moral equality among human beings, pro-life activists and scholars have defended the traditional ethic. The decline of the old ethic has created a moral vacuum, however, and there have been scores of suggestions about what the new morality will or should look like. Although many have tried to create a workable performance-based theory of moral personhood to fill the ethical void, others have simply dispensed with the inquiry into personhood altogether.

## KILLING PERSONS

The most famous and influential justification of this sort comes from Thomson's 1971 article "In Defense of Abortion."[66] For the sake of argument, Thomson conceded the premise that "the fetus is a human being, a person, from the moment of conception."[67] Still, by way of a thought experiment, Thomson argued that fetal personhood did not make abortion morally impermissible. "[L]et me ask you to imagine this," Thomson wrote,

[65] Kavanaugh, *Who Counts as Persons?*, 68.
[66] Judith Jarvis Thomson, "In Defense of Abortion," *Philosophy & Public Affairs* 1, no. 1 (1971), 47–66.
[67] Ibid., 47. Although she thought the "premise is false," Thomson nonetheless acknowledged, "we shall probably have to agree that the fetus has already become a human person well before birth" (47–48).

You wake up in the morning and find yourself back to back in bed with an unconscious violinist. A famous unconscious violinist. He has been found to have a fatal kidney ailment, and the Society of Music Lovers has canvassed all the available medical records and found that you alone have the right blood type to help. They have therefore kidnapped you, and last night the violinist's circulatory system was plugged into yours, so that your kidneys can be used to extract poisons from his blood as well as your own. The director of the hospital now tells you, "Look, we're sorry the Society of Music Lovers did this to you – we would never have permitted it if we had known. But, still, they did it, and the violinist is plugged into you. To unplug you would be to kill him. But never mind, it's only for nine months. By then he will have recovered from his ailment, and can safely be unplugged from you." Is it morally incumbent on you to accede to this situation? No doubt it would be very nice of you if you did, a great kindness. But do you *have* to accede to it? What if it were not nine months, but nine years? Or longer still? What if the director of the hospital says, "Tough luck, I agree, but you've now got to stay in bed, with the violinist plugged into you, for the rest of your life. Because remember this. All persons have a right to life, and violinists are persons. Granted you have a right to decide what happens in and to your body, but a person's right to life outweighs your right to decide what happens in and to your body. So you cannot ever be unplugged from him."[68]

Thomson's thought experiment was, of course, designed to make the case that there is something intuitively wrong with requiring one person to involuntarily give up use of her body to another person, even if such use is necessary to preserve the latter person's life. With respect to abortion, then, the question of personhood would seem to be irrelevant, for the unborn child would have no "right" to use her mother's body against her will. As Eileen McDonagh explains, "the woman may defend herself against nonconsensual intrusion of a fetus on her bodily integrity and liberty just as she would have the right to defend herself against the nonconsensual intrusion of a dying violinist."[69]

---

[68] Ibid., 49.

[69] Eileen McDonagh, "The Case of the Missing Frame: Abortion as Self-Defense," *Historical Methods* 40, no. 4 (2007), 190. See also McDonagh's *Breaking the Abortion Deadlock: From Choice to Consent* (New York: Oxford University Press, 1996), which expands Thomson's argument into the domain of constitutional law.

Of course, the thought experiment can be changed to tap into other intuitions. What if the violinist was your child? And what if the only way to "unplug" her was by suffocating or decapitating her? Or, from a different angle, what if technological developments made it so that one could be "unplugged" from the violinist without killing her? Does a right to unplug one's self from the violinist necessitate a right to seek the violinist's death? This question is particularly troubling for modern defenders of abortion choice, because technological advancements have made it more plausible that one day we will be able to fully dissociate abortion from killing. If a woman could simply "unplug" herself from her unborn child *and* keep the child alive, would this dissolve the moral dispute? Apparently not: As Soran Reader argues, the "feminist presumption is that abortion must end the life of the fetus, since this is what women seek when they seek abortions. Women seeking abortion do not want to give up their fetus; they want to ensure that there is no being in the world to whom they are related as mother to child."[70] And, of course, this unavoidably leads back to the ethics of infanticide, since Reader also argues women "have a moral right to secure the death of the fetus once it is out of their body."[71]

After forty years of argument and debate about the ethics and legality of abortion, we remain at an impasse. What makes the gulf between the contending sides seem unbridgeable is that in moments of candor all agree that abortion involves the deliberate destruction of a human life. Arguments in defense of this destruction either define personhood in such a way as to exclude the unborn (and sometimes the newly born) or simply defend abortion (and sometimes infanticide) as the justifiable killing of a person. Both defenses of abortion have in common a

---

[70] Soran Reader, "Abortion, Killing, and Maternal Moral Authority," *Hypatia* 23, no. 1 (2008), 134.
[71] Ibid., 134.

rejection of the moral tradition underpinning our shared notions of equality and natural rights. If human beings are equal in a fundamental moral sense, and if human beings really are endowed with certain inalienable rights, then killing in abortion cannot so easily be distinguished from killing in other circumstances. From this perspective, it is easy to see why many people today speak as the nineteenth-century physicians spoke, calling abortion "murder," "unborn-child-killing," and the like. But "say that often and loudly enough," Thomson warned, "and some weak-minded soul is sure to start shooting to put a stop to it."[72] Tragically, some weak-minded souls have used bombs and guns in an attempt to stop abortion, and the periodic outbursts of violence against abortion doctors introduce a final, tragic dimension to the parallels between abortion and slavery.

## THE DARK SIDE OF ABOLITION

On Pentecost Sunday, 2009, Scott Roeder entered the foyer of Wichita's Reformation Lutheran Church and put a single bullet in the forehead of George Tiller, a sixty-seven-year-old late-term abortion provider who had long drawn the ire of pro-life activists. In the midst of the ensuing media frenzy, Roeder immediately claimed the mantle of nineteenth-century abolitionist John Brown, a fellow evangelical Christian who hailed from the same American heartland.[73] Roeder did resemble Brown at least in this: Both believed "the crimes of this *guilty land*: will never be purged *away*; but with *Blood*."[74] Tiller's death marked the fourth targeted assassination of an abortion doctor since 1993 and the eighth total fatality

---

[72] Thomson, "Abortion," *Boston Review* (1995).

[73] See Roxana Hegeman, "Abortion Doctor's Killer Says He Has No Regrets," *Associated Press* (10 February 2010).

[74] Letter of John Brown (2 December 1859), as quoted in Richard J. Hinton, *John Brown and His Men* (New York: Funk and Wagnalls Co., 1894), 398.

caused by anti-abortion violence.[75] Although the condemnation of Roeder's vigilantism was immediate and uniform across most of America (including every prominent pro-life organization), Roeder – now serving a life sentence – continues to enjoy the support of a small group of committed activists affiliated with a loose-knit anti-abortion organization known as the Army of God.[76]

One of those activists is Michael Bray, a Lutheran minister who spent four years in a federal penitentiary for a series of abortion clinic bombings in the 1980s.[77] Bray also made a name for himself in militant anti-abortion circles with his 1993 book *A Time to Kill*. The book provides the classic apology for anti-abortion violence, and it continues to serve as a theological primer of sorts for Christians who condone lethal force as a morally licit means of protesting the injustice of abortion. As political scientist Jon Shields notes, "what distinguishes pro-life bombers and assassins" such as Roeder from the mainstream pro-life movement "is not the degree of their moral conviction, but their fanatical commitment to a certain understanding of political theology."[78] Reverend Bray has contributed to this political theology by arguing that the use of lethal force in the fight against abortion can appropriately be situated within Christendom's just war tradition. "The Christian just war theory," Bray writes, "was built not upon a principle of self-defense, but upon that of defense of another. Accordingly, force may be lawfully wielded by the Christian authorized by the state, or by the private citizen authorized as it were

---

[75] These numbers are according to records kept by the National Abortion Federation. See http://www.prochoice.org/about_abortion/violence/history_vio lence.html.

[76] For a general overview of the organization, see Jennifer Jefferis, *Armed for Life: The Army of God and Anti-Abortion Terror in the United States* (Santa Barbara, CA: ABC-CLIO, 2011).

[77] For a historical treatment of Bray's turn to violence, see James Risen and Judy L. Thomas, *Wrath of Angels: The American Abortion War* (New York: Basic Books, 1998), 78–100.

[78] Jon A. Shields, "What Abortionist Killers Believe," *The Weekly Standard* 14, no. 38 (June 22, 2009).

by God (and in fact most states of the United States) for the purpose of protecting a neighbor from harm."[79] Bray – like many radical activists before him – looks to the rebel slaves and violent abolitionists of the past for solidarity and support. Nat Turner, Joseph Cinque, Denmark Vesey, and John Brown all used deadly force to combat the evils of slavery, Bray notes, and he sees himself as an heir to this tradition of radical abolitionism and dissent. He appeals in particular to John Brown, the fiery anti-slavery radical who was executed for his failed 1859 raid on the federal arsenal at Harper's Ferry, Virginia. There is a clear resemblance, Bray insists, between today's anti-abortion vigilantes and the radical abolitionists of the nineteenth century. The claimed connection is perhaps strengthened by the initial public reaction to the loss of life – some eighteen casualties, including several bystanders – occasioned by the raid on Harper's Ferry. "I read all the newspapers I could within a week after this event," Henry David Thoreau recollected shortly after the raid, "and I do not remember in them a single expression of sympathy for these men. ... Even [the anti-slavery] *Liberator* called it a 'misguided, wild, and apparently insane effort.'"[80]

Bray, however – like Thoreau – lionizes John Brown as a prophet and a martyr, and he draws three interrelated lessons from Brown's life and death. First, "Those who function in a prophetic role are small in number, for the majority of the population in times of general apostasy are well duped by the spirit of the age."[81] Second, "When a population grows accustomed to an evil; when, in fact, the evil is institutionalized, opponents appear more and more strange. Eccentrics. Extremists."[82] Finally, "The evil of

[79] Michael Bray, *A Time to Kill: A Study Concerning the Use of Force and Abortion* (Portland, OR: Advocates for Life Publications, 1994), 67.

[80] Henry David Thoreau, "A Plea for Captain Brown," in James Redpath, *Echoes of Harper's Ferry* (Boston: Thayer and Eldridge, 1860), 17–43. Cited in Bray, *A Time to Kill*, 90–91.

[81] Bray, *A Time to Kill*, 92.

[82] Ibid., 92.

one's own time is difficult to discern because of the attendant duty to resist it."[83] Of course, many pro-life activists would agree with all three of these lessons. But, according to Bray, the mainstream pro-life movement is deeply misguided in its advocacy of moral suasion, political reform, and nonviolent protest. On this score, Bray's argument is straightforward. He insists there is no difference in principle between the private use of force – even *lethal* force – to obstruct the operations of an abortion clinic and the private use of force to protect a child (or any other person) from a deadly assault. The challenge Bray levels at pro-life activists is thus put in the form of a question: "How does one (1) hold a principle of self-defense and the defense of others, (2) affirm the extreme of war as an extension of that principle, (3) affirm that the preborn are innocent people deserving protection, and then (4) deny that these people ought to be afforded even basic forceful defense?"[84]

## SLAVERY, ABORTION, AND THE ETHICS OF LIFE

The mainstream pro-life movement is divided in its response to Bray's challenge, but there are essentially two common answers: *either* (1) it is never morally permissible to deliberately will the death of another human being *or* (2) only public authority can properly wield the power of the sword.[85] In either case, the moral legitimacy of private vigilantism is ruled out from the start. The first answer echoes abolitionist William Lloyd Garrison's assertion (in response to John Brown's raid) that he continued to believe in "the inviolability of human life, under all

---

[83] Ibid., 95.
[84] Ibid., 78.
[85] These two responses were each represented in a controversial symposium on the ethics of killing abortion doctors in a 1994 issue of the journal *First Things*. See "Killing Abortionists: A Symposium," *First Things* (December 1994), http://www.firstthings.com/article/2007/01/killing-abortionists-a-symposium-31.

circumstances."[86] Such a belief would absolutely and unequivocally condemn the murder of an abortion doctor.

As John Kavanaugh writes, the moral inviolability of human life "yields the root prohibition against the direct intentional killing of any human being" – a "highly demanding" moral standard that has the virtue of being "direct and concise."[87] Still, in our own day, as in Garrison's, few truly believe in the inviolability of human life in all circumstances. The second common response thus holds out the possibility of just intentional killing by duly constituted public authorities in carefully defined circumstances but condemns the man who commits private acts of violence, a formula that also yields an unequivocal and absolute condemnation of the murder of abortion doctors.[88]

In either ethical paradigm, the "killing of an abortionist," as Nat Hentoff observed, "makes one the mirror image of the abortionist."[89] One of Bray's other heroes, however, provides an example of what many would be tempted to consider a just use of private lethal force in the service of a righteous cause.[90] During World War II, the young German theologian and pastor Dietrich Bonhoeffer participated in a failed plot to assassinate Adolf Hitler. After his arrest and trial Bonhoeffer was hanged by the Third Reich, but he remains for many "a martyr whose actions appear to legitimate acts of individual violence done by others for

---

[86] William Lloyd Garrison, "Speech of William Lloyd Garrison," *Liberator* (December 16, 1859), 198.

[87] John F. Kavanaugh, *Who Counts as Persons?*, 119. Kavanaugh analyzes the case of self-defense against an aggressor and the use of force in a just war through the lens of "double effect," a philosophical doctrine that would allow death to occur through otherwise justified actions provided death was not directly intended. See pp. 122–125.

[88] See, for example, G. J. McAleer, *To Kill Another: Homicide and Natural Law* (New Brunswick, NJ: Transaction Publishers, 2010). McAleer's thesis, following Aquinas and Suarez, is that "only public authority has the privilege to intentionally kill" (ix). Cf. Aquinas, *S.T.*, II-II, 63.3.

[89] "Killing Abortionists: A Symposium," *First Things* (December 1994).

[90] See Bray, *A Time to Kill*, 96.

allegedly Christian reasons."[91] Yet as the editor of the
English edition of Bonhoeffer's *Ethics* comments,

> those who appeal to Bonhoeffer's participation in the conspiracy to
> kill Hitler to justify their violence, for example, attacking doctors
> who perform abortions, are in fact invoking Bonhoeffer *against*
> themselves. Bonhoeffer's position was supported by the tyranni-
> cide tradition in Christian ethics. He represented a moral consensus
> and was not a self-appointed vigilante. He did not consider his
> agreement to killing Hitler a principle that could be extrapolated.
> And he judged Hitler's genocidal regime a threat to the very social
> order sustaining life. Such a constellation is rarely transferable.[92]

Bonhoeffer's specific discussion of abortion also weighs
against appealing to his authority to justify private violence
against abortion doctors. Although unambiguous in his
moral condemnation of abortion – he insisted the act was
"nothing but murder"[93] – Bonhoeffer's response to the
problem of abortion was moderated by his acknowledg-
ment of the issue's complexity. "Various motives may lead
to such an act," he noted.

> It may be a deed of despair from the depths of human desolation or
> financial need, in which case guilt falls often more on the commun-
> ity than on the individual. It may be that on this very point money
> can cover over a great deal of careless behavior, whereas among the
> poor even the deed done with great reluctance comes more easily
> to light. Without doubt, all this decisively affects one's personal,
> pastoral attitude toward the person concerned; but it cannot
> change the fact of murder.[94]

It is, in this context, impossible to imagine Bonhoeffer coun-
seling a would-be Scott Roeder to execute an abortion doctor
in the name of Christian charity, no matter how forcefully he
denounced the act of abortion itself.

Nevertheless, as Simon Schama comments, the way
nineteenth-century evangelical abolitionists approached the

---

[91] Clifford J. Green, "Pacifism and Tyrannicide: Bonhoeffer's Christian Peace
Ethic," *Studies in Christian Ethics* 18, no. 31 (2005), 32.
[92] *Dietrich Bonhoeffer Works, Volume 6: Ethics*, Clifford J. Green, trans. and ed.
(Minneapolis, MN: Fortress Press, 2005), 25 n. 98.
[93] Ibid., 206.
[94] Ibid., 207.

issue of slavery is "not altogether different from the way Right to Life evangelicals argue today."⁹⁵ The same can be said of the violent wings of both reform movements, and the suggestive title of the concluding section in *A Time to Kill* – "The New Abolitionists" – thus adds a final tragic layer to the parallel politics of slavery and abortion. Of course, the jurisprudential, historical, and philosophical connections are complex and never entirely congruent. It is therefore important to think clearly about the ways in which these two issues are and are *not* alike, and the most important practical way these issues differ – a point that demands emphasis in light of the intermittent acts of violence that continue to plague the anti-abortion movement – is that abortion cannot and will not be settled by violence or armed conflict. There is no geographic line or sectional interest associated with abortion, and the culture itself remains deeply ambivalent about its resolution.

Across the political spectrum people share a visceral reaction to violence done to fetuses who have recognizably human traits, but very few people have the same response to the destruction of a zygote or early embryo. "Viewed in this light," Shields concludes, "emotion is driving moderate – not extreme – public opinion."⁹⁶ Still, the most coherent arguments in academic bioethics remain at one of two extremes. Either human status (irrespective of anthropomorphic characteristics) supplies the grounds of human dignity and worth *or* some extrinsic characteristic such as self-consciousness confers individual moral status at a stage of development some time *after* birth. Each of these positions rests on technical philosophical arguments that are at odds with the modal sentiments of the population at large. Instead of black and white, many people see shades of gray. Ambiguity obscures the principles that are at

---

⁹⁵ Simon Schama, *The American Future: A History* (New York: HarperCollins, 2010), 183.
⁹⁶ Jon A. Shields, "Almost Human: Ambivalence in the Pro-Choice and Pro-Life Movements," *Critical Review* 23, no. 4 (2011), 512.

stake and, for many, makes the frequently alleged analogy between abortion and slavery seem quaint and idiosyncratic.

The perpetual tension between our reason and our sentiments may perhaps give us cause to doubt that our society will ever look back on abortion – at least at the very earliest stages of pregnancy – with the same horror that we have for slavery. Indeed, there is a felt absurdity to the claim that zygotes and early embryos are full members of our species deserving of the same protection and respect as anyone else, and this sentiment moderates even the pro-life movement. As Eric Cohen noted in the pages of *The New Atlantis*, however, our emotional and aesthetic sensitivity to physical characteristics that develop on a continuum during (and after) pregnancy "is not very rational. It is surely not a scientific argument grounded in biology, but a moral feeling about who is equal and who is not."[97] Cohen's observation does not lessen the feeling, but it does offer rational grounds to question it.

At the dawn of the twenty-first century, the particularly pressing question of the moral status of the embryo has also renewed serious debate about the lessons to be gleaned from the history of American slavery. In his foreword to a report on human cloning issued by the President's Council on Bioethics, Leon Kass comments,

> with slavery or despotism, it is easy to identify evil as evil, and the challenge is rather to figure out how best to combat it. But in the realm of bioethics, the evils we face (if indeed they are evils) are intertwined with the goods we so keenly seek: cures for disease, relief of suffering, and preservation of life. When good and bad are so intermixed, distinguishing between them is often extremely difficult.[98]

Yet Kass' student, Diana Schaub, offered an important historical qualification to the comparison between the new

---

[97] Eric Cohen, "The Tragedy of Equality," *The New Atlantis* (Fall 2004/Winter 2005), 106.

[98] Leon Kass, foreword to *Human Cloning and Human Dignity: The Report of the President's Council on Bioethics* (New York: Perseus Books, 2002), xv–xvi.

bioethical challenges and slavery. It "was not at all easy," she pointed out, "to bring men to see slavery as evil, particularly not once the practice of slavery was well-established in the life of the nation."[99] In the same way, it is not at all easy to bring people to see the evil of creating and destroying human lives, particularly when the promise of curing disease or ending suffering or ensuring equality is held out as a justification. Still, what is at stake in some of our current bioethical debates is the creation, ownership, destruction, and private use of nascent human beings. This new field of inquiry moves us beyond the familiar "abortion is like slavery" analogy; in our brave new world, we are confronted in a real sense with "slavery *plus* abortion."[100] As we continue to wrestle with the fundamental questions at the heart of the struggle over American slavery, these new challenges will force us to consider again the truth and relevance of what Lincoln simply called the "sheet anchor of American republicanism": a belief, declared in the nation's infancy, that all human beings are created equal and endowed by their Creator with certain unalienable rights.[101]

---

[99] Diana Schaub, "Slavery plus Abortion," *The Public Interest* (Winter 2003), 46.
[100] Ibid.
[101] Basler, ed., *Collected Works of Abraham Lincoln*, Vol. 2, 266.

# Index